THINK LIKE A WHITE MAN

THINK LIKE A WHITE MAN

A SATIRICAL GUIDE TO CONQUERING THE WORLD . . . WHILE BLACK

Dr BOULÉ WHYTELAW III
PROFESSOR OF WHITE PEOPLE STUDIES

(AS TOLD TO NELS ABBEY)

CANONGATE

This paperback edition published in 2020 by Canongate Books

First published in Great Britain, the USA and Canada in 2019
by Canongate Books Ltd, 14 High Street, Edinburgh EH1 1TE

Distributed in the USA by Publishers Group West and in
Canada by Publishers Group Canada

canongate.co.uk

1

Quotation from speech by Lucius Cary, 15th Viscount Falkland in
The Official Record of the Debate Initiated by Lord Gifford QC in
the House of Lords of the British Parliament on 14th March 1996
Concerning the African Reparations, col. 1052.

Extract from *The Huey P. Newton Reader* © Huey Newton, 2002.
Reprinted with permission of Seven Stories Press.

British Library Cataloguing-in-Publication Data
A catalogue record for this book is available on
request from the British Library

ISBN 978 1 78689 440 3

Typeset in Sabon by e-type

Printed and bound in Great Britain by Clays Ltd, Elcograf S.p.A.

About the Authors

Dr Boulé Whytelaw III

Dr Boulé Whytelaw III is the Distinguished Professor of White People Studies at Bishop Lamonthood University, the Deputy Vice Chair of the C(T)UWP, the Centre for (Trying to) Understand White People, and is widely acknowledged as the definitive global authority on white people.

He is the highly accomplished television-writing brain behind the hit shows *Good Cops, Good White Folk and Other Wild Fantasies* and *Scientific Proof: The White Man's Ice Is Indeed Colder.*

Prior to an unfortunate redundancy he was a decorated banker (specialising in no-income, no-job or assets loans) and a grandee of a slew of corporate diversity schemes.

Nels Abbey

Nels Abbey is a British Nigerian (Itsekiri) writer and media executive based in London. This is his first book.

I dedicate this book to the most precious group of beings on the face of the Earth, as well as the foremost resistors of White-Manism: black women. Sistas, you're loved, admired and worshipped by me. Forever and a day. You're deeply appreciated.

I also dedicate this book to my amazing white wife.

– Dr Boulé Whytelaw III

Contents

PART 1: UNDERSTANDING THE WHITE MAN

PART 2: OVERTHROWING THE WHITE MAN

Introduction

Nels Abbey

D r Boulé (pronounced *boo-lay*) Fabricius Whytelaw III was born Blakamoor-Tajudeeni Mamasay-Mamakusa somewhere in the early 70s (by my estimations). In order to achieve what he called 'white success' he changed his name to sound as white as possible (not dissimilar – as he would inform me – to Charlie Sheen, Ralph Lauren and Whoopi Goldberg).[1]

After this slight relabelling, he started getting job interviews and eventually an offer that was unthinkable to a black person called 'Blakamoor-Tajudeeni' (this was long before brands like 'Barack Obama' and 'Lupita Nyong'o' successfully emerged). This experience made him realise that making himself as palatable to white people as possible would help propel him to 'white success'. He felt the need to go further. Much further.

He began to study Caucasians, in his words, 'from Austria to Australia, London to Los Angeles, Cape Town to the Caucasus Mountains, Whitehall to the White House and everywhere white in-between'. He earned a PhD in White People Studies (the first and only human I am aware of to do so) and emerged as the foremost expert on 'the world's toughest subject: white people'.

Clearly a Westerner born to African parents, though he was reluctant to divulge exactly where he was from, the good

1 Born, respectively, Carlos Irwin Estévez, Ralph Lifshitz and Caryn Elaine Johnson.

doctor is what many would call a 'global citizen', or what the British Prime Minister Theresa May would call a 'citizen of nowhere'. His politics, his outlook on the world and his diction all reflect this.

Out of the clear blue sky, Dr Whytelaw contacted me in early 2014 to help him package and share his message on how 'we' – by which he meant 'black people' – transit from 'civil rights to silver rights … from marching to money-making … from fighting for freedom to actual freedom'. He explained that he had the 'blueprint to overthrow the White Man [not to be mistaken for a "white man", he stresses] once and for all'. When I asked for brief details, he elaborated: 'We will use the White Man's own weapons and tools to defeat him and we will start in the whitest place possible: the corporate world.'

I pointed out the wise words of the great poet Audre Lorde: 'the master's tools will never dismantle the master's house'. After a long and frustrated pause Dr Whytelaw responded: 'Nigga, you sound like an idiot or, even worse, a poet. Why would we want to dismantle a house we built? We don't want to dismantle anything, we want to throw the blue-eyed squatter out and live in it ourselves.'

On the back of the statement above, I made it clear that I despise the N-word and would rather he didn't use it around me. His response: 'Nigga, nigga, nigga, nigga, nigga, nigga, nigga. I've held back my language and repressed myself all my life. And what did it earn me? Anxiety, high blood pressure and, fair enough, a lot of money. Anyway, nigga, I will use whatever word keeps me alive, happy and wealthy.'

How he got my details remains a mystery to me. Nevertheless, after months of trying to convince me that there is no such thing as a 'white fatwa', he got me to agree to help bring his vision to life.

Dr Whytelaw is a fascinating person. An unhinged black man with no political filter or time for political correctness whatsoever – a degree of freedom I would normally only associate with the most comfortable of comfortable white men. A truly unique compendium of racial knowledge and insight. Charming, witty, forthright and, according to him, 'always right'.

During moments of creative and racial disagreement he would firmly reassure me that he 'is to white people what Warren Buffet is to stocks, what Bill Gates is to computers, what Colonel Sanders is to stealing secret recipes from black women ...' And rightly so. He is an authority, and his theories (which he would demand I label 'facts') are nothing short of ground-breaking.

In early February 2019, Dr Whytelaw texted me to say he was about to embark on an 'urgent scientific field trip' to 'discover, research and document' a 'remote white tribe'. No one has heard from him since.

This book is the fruit of all the discussions, lessons and ideas which emerged from hundreds of hours of meetings with Dr Whytelaw. This is his gift to the world, even though much of the hard work was mine.

HOWEVER, PLEASE NOTE THAT ABSOLUTELY NONE OF THE OPINIONS, THOUGHTS OR ADVICE OFFERED IN THIS BOOK ARE MINE OR ANYTHING TO DO WITH ME.

I'm only in this for the money.

Assumptions

This book is written with the following assumptions about you, the reader:

1. You are classified as black:

- Meaning you were born with at least a single drop of wild black African blood in your veins which has physically manifested itself in you (e.g. brown skin, impressive genitalia, natural rhythm, a proneness to police brutality, punctuality issues, healthy distrust of people classified as white, etc.).

- You do not have a gang tattoo on your face, a catalogue of violent or pornographic YouTube videos or a lengthy criminal record owing to a former career in rap music.

- You are a professional (or you aspire to be one) and therefore have an intimate understanding of the necessity of Prozac (or aspire to such an understanding).

- You *can* handle the truth.

2. In the event you are not (blessed enough to be) classified as black:

- You are a voyeur of black people for personal, professional, political, perverted or policing reasons

Or

- You're just some bored racist devil.

Preamble

Brace Yourself ...

'I'm terribly sorry. What I'm about to say is something so racist I never thought my soul could ever feel it. But I truly never wanna spend time with white people again ...'

– Sinéad O'Connor

I wasn't always the pillar of wisdom that I am today. Far from it. Once upon a time I was just like you: young, dumb and ... living with Mum.

I used to believe that I would flourish if I just worked multiple times as hard as my white peers (as Mama used to say). I used to believe in a fair and equitable corporate world: almost a Disneyland of meritocracies; I used to believe that the concept of a racial caste system was something that existed only in the backwaters of India and history books. I also used to believe in Father Christmas, the Tooth Fairy, Mary Poppins, Tony Blair and a slew of other dubious white characters.

Of all the tomfoolery listed above, I'm least ashamed of the last sentence (other than the Tony Blair stuff, which really was naïve: should have seen *that* White Man coming). I was a happy fool, a Jonestown Kool-Aid sipper; a 'change we can believe in'-er, if you will. Then I managed to break into the corporate world ...

Straight outta university, straight into a mountain of debt and uncertainty, full of determination and armed with a degree, I was ready for the world, ready for my giant leap forward. One 'minor' challenge: I was an ambitious black person in a racism-riddled white-dominated society. And a black person with an education, a well-rehearsed polished accent and no criminal record is still a black person, still a nigger.

I would offer details of my rats, roaches and racism-riddled childhood and tell you how hard it was for my family and how we suffered and struggled. But that's as predictable as top black athletes marrying austere, entry-level white women and going broke within weeks of their careers ending. Plus, if white corporate life in thick black skin has taught me anything, it's that no one cares how hard you had it. Screw your sob story: it's little more than comedy fodder. And, if you're not careful, so is your career.

Nevertheless, to manage expectations:

- No, I wasn't raised by wild bears in the woods. My mother wasn't a crack-addicted prostitute.[1] And my father was not a hustler with a life worthy of a Lee Daniels epic.

- No, I never sold, transported or took drugs. I'd never even seen drugs in real life until I started working with 'well-adjusted' white people.

- No, I am not able to run 100m under a minute or cross a football onto another man's waiting head or dunk a basketball.

- And no, I never got kicked or dropped out of school. In fact, I never even stabbed or knee-capped a supply teacher.

1 Although that would have been ideal if I'd been on a quest for success as a creative because nothing, absolutely nothing, propels a black-centred piece of art or literature to prominence like a Nazi-lite black mother clutching a crack pipe with her dark crusty lips while beating the black out of her children. See *Precious*, *Moonlight*, *Menace II Society* and *Monster's Ball* for examples.

And neither had anyone in my family. Even if we had, that wouldn't have been our biggest sin. For as far as society was, and is, concerned, our sins – the sins of my family and people like us – were much greater than all of these combined. We were much more serious a plague than, say, mumble rappers, global warming or even vegan hipsters: we were immigrants.

Black African immigrants. The exact type of black people white do-gooder types would feel the need to take a Comic Relief-style picture with. The lowest of the low. Let in to the country to 'do the jobs *our people* don't want to do'.

We – and those like us who didn't qualify as *our people* (usually people with brown skin weirdly described as 'black') – cleaned a lot of toilets, swept a lot of roads, manned a lot of doors, fled a lot of immigration officials and kissed, sucked and wiped a lot of white ass. That was your place, and you'd better be happy with it. Or you could fuck off back to Mudhutistan.

So, after a childhood witnessing that pandemonium, I was determined to see to it that I emerged above cattle class. I wanted what had eluded us all along: to be middle-class, white-collar and paid-like-a-White Man; to be a professional, a contender within society, a winner. I wanted this so badly that I was willing to achieve it by any means necessary. I was happy to die trying – well, not really, but it makes for a hell of a catchy phrase. The problem, I learnt, for black professionals is that 'succeed or die trying' is not just a hyper masculine 50 Cent-inspired catchphrase: it is real. If your body and soul don't part ways during the struggle, your mind and sanity almost certainly will.

I made a few minor adjustments to my identity – slight alteration to my name, changed address to a white friend's place who lived in a more desirable area, started wearing a wedding ring despite being single, wore glasses though I have perfect eyesight – general stuff that helps white people feel more relaxed around black people, and eventually, after hundreds of applications and hundreds of rejection letters, humiliation, fake smiles and patronising nods, I was offered a job – a job with one of the best firms in the world, in fact. A firm whose very name was synonymous with integrity, profitability, professionalism and, most importantly, long-distance-jogging white people in expensive attire.

And as any remotely sane black person knows: where there are salad-loving and long-distance-jogging white people in expensive attire there is money to be made.[2]

Screw the glass ceiling; I'd cheated on fate. Hallelujah! Halle Berry! Show me the motherfucking hard-cold cash money! I've made it.

Such were my youthful thoughts.

I woke up to my first day on the job feeling the excitement a rosy-cheeked spoilt white child goes to bed with on Christmas Eve. I said my prayers with a smile and tears of joy running down my face and walked into the living room to meet my father ironing my clothes, something he hadn't done in … ever. I took a shower and spent around five minutes in the mirror making sure my waves were tight.[3] I threw on my suit and tie. And then my shoes. I looked open-casket sharp.

'Let's do this,' I said to myself.

As I flung open my bedroom door to leave, my entire family was standing there, waiting for me with pride in their eyes. They quietly shuffled into my room. My mother asked me to drop to my knees. The family each put a hand on me and

2 Wealth generation tip: if you are trying to sell a residential property, hire white people to jog back and forth round the property whenever a viewing is scheduled. I estimate that 'jogging white people' add 15% to the value of any property.

3 Keeping YT in the loop, 'waves' are a difficult-to-achieve and even-harder-to-maintain sex-magnet black hairstyle in which short black hairs curl on top and into each other to form a pattern that looks like ocean waves. Appropriation attempts will prove futile.

prayed (not entirely dissimilar to what black payola prosti-
tute-pastors do for racist politicians during elections).[4]

As I left, my mother offered some advice: 'You have to work
twice as hard as everyone else. Don't forget where you came
from. Don't forget who you are.'

And with those wise words/clichés ringing in my ears, a lot
of Jesus and the warm wishes of my family, I left to take on
the world: the white corporate world.

I was due to start at 9.30, so of course I arrived an hour
early – this is known as transcending via racism-driven low
expectations – and was kept waiting eagerly in the immaculate
reception, complete with awe-inspiring fountain.

The lovely receptionist invited me to take a seat but I decided
to stand up while waiting. I thought it gave a better indication
of my seriousness and focus. Like a colonial governor general
with a head full of white supremacy (and a body full of lust for
anything in black skin), I meant business and I wanted to let it
be known to the 'natives'.

Two men who looked eye-wateringly rich and white – at
the time, interchangeable terms to me – were talking to each
other as they walked in. They saw me, stopped and said,
'Good morning.' Friendly, I thought. Then they started to pat
themselves down looking for something as they stood in front
of me. Much to his personal relief, one of the men found what
he was looking for in his wallet.

'I thought I left it at home … there you go, mate,' he said as
he showed me his company identity card. His colleague found
his and did the same. So did the next few people coming in
after them. From there it snowballed; almost everyone showed
me their identity cards as they passed by. Some would greet

4 Feel free to do an internet search using the words 'Donald Trump black
pastors'.

me, others wouldn't even make eye contact, yet they all showed me their ID cards.

The naïve feeling of having broken into the white corporate world had lulled me into a false sense of security, so I was initially confused. Then it clicked: how could I forget? I'm black! They thought I was a security guard. A brother in a suit in such an environment is usually only there for a range of plausible reasons: manning the door, giving talks on 'the importance of diversity', wringing bleeding white hearts for cash for his latest youth-mentoring scheme or providing barely legal gigolo services to some bitter white divorcee.

As embarrassing as the realisation was, even this didn't dent my enthusiasm. I was there for my expertise and intellectual prowess. I belonged there as much as they did. I was as good as them and soon I'd prove myself their better. On the bright side, no one tried to tip me. I often wonder if I would have accepted the tip if they had: I was as broke as Greece after all.

And then *she* turned up in all her *Fox News*-peroxide glory, smiling like that beautiful intersection between an abolitionist and a capitalist. Dripping with middle-class whiteness, Sarah[5] the Sloane Ranger, my first ever boss, arrived to welcome me to the firm.

Luckily for my newbie zeal, my closet-racist-radar (or, as I call it now, my 'shy Trump Voter/Brexiter detector') didn't go off in Sarah's presence. She felt like a genuinely nice, non-racist white person (i.e. a bearable white person who probably grew up listening to Brand Nubian and Public Enemy and embraced the anti-white supremacy rhetoric). We kibitzed warmly as she took me to meet the rest of the department.

The lift door opened and, whooosh, welcome to Caucasiastan.

---

5 Reminder: all names in this book have been changed to protect the treacherously litigious.

I hadn't seen that much white since the last time I watched the final scenes of *Scarface*. All 116 of my new colleagues were white. Very white. Whiter than a pre-Meghan Markle royal wedding. Or a Richard Ayoade film.

My black-dar didn't register a single blip. There was not a discernible fraction of a drop of black blood in the room. No Tom Jones-like suspicious curls, no marginally wider than expected nostrils, no dubiously brown eyes and no slightly olive skin. Absolutely no sign that white mummy may have bagged herself a reefer-smoking Barack Obama[6] in a bar one lonely night and unleashed her love for the hot cocoa on him. And in the interest of balance, there was no sign that white daddy met a sister and got his Thomas Jefferson on, either. No quadroon cousin passing for a Sicilian sibling. Nothing. The company was as white as post-gentrification Brixton.

This should have been surprising, given the oft-touted 'rich' diversity of the city where the company was based, but it wasn't: I had expected that to be the case. The only diversity that concerned such firms at the time was – and still is – likely to be in an investment portfolio or a pack of M&Ms. Anything other than that: 'Pristine virgin Aryan white, please. Thank you.'

Later on that morning, I was dispatched to go and attend a few hours of induction training. We were warmly welcomed and went through the usual jarring motions of enthusiastically introducing ourselves and profiling each other based on our hierarchy within the company. And then came the obligatory corporate propaganda video.

As the short film was about to start, a young man with a distinct Australian accent rushed into the room and sat beside me.

6 More info on Barack Obama's marijuana smoking days with the 'Choom Gang' here: https://www.telegraph.co.uk/news/worldnews/barackobama/9290972/Barack-Obamas-marijuana-smoking-days-with-the-Choom-Gang.html.

'Sorry I'm late. Sorry I'm late. Aussie People's Time! Aussie People's Time!' he said, evoking a chuckle from the room as the lights dimmed for the video.

When the corporate porn ended I started speaking to the Aussie guy. He seemed like a nice chap and we struck a chord. Feeling that profoundly black urge to prove that I was there on merit, I carefully explained my qualifications and background and what I'd be doing. I then learned that he'd be working in the same department as me, but in a different and far more desirable and lucrative role. Anyway, having shown him mine, I naturally wanted to see his. So, I asked where and what he studied at university.

'University? Now that's a big word from a big fella. No university for me. I didn't have time for that, mate. I left school at fifteen, did the odd job here and there, but I've mostly been travelling for the last few years. Sold fish and chips on the beach in Cornwall for the last couple of weeks and here I am,' he explained.

And there it was. He had no qualifications, no experience and had only been in the country a couple of weeks. Yet he was in a position I and my more qualified noir-as-fuck friends and family would have given a kidney (or two) to be in.

The parts of my family who were not shipped round the globe for enslavement purposes were, a few quick centuries later, conscripted from 'the colonies' (i.e. their own land that white people had at the time stolen), moved to different parts of the world to fight white-on-white tribal conflicts (popularly known as World Wars) that had nothing to do with them, and spent forty years in the West in seemingly inescapable poverty and the modern equivalent of indentured servitude for me to get a foot in the door of the corporate world. No matter the qualifications we had – these are Africans we are talking about here: they had more degrees than a thermometer – we just didn't seem to 'qualify'. Yet kangaroo-humping Crocodile Dundee rocks up and gets a choice job in a week?

As my days, months and years of corporate experience accumulated I learned that this was no fluke or exception to the norm. This *was* the norm. It didn't end at recruitment (it didn't begin there, either). It seeped right the way through corporate life. In fact, it seeped right the way through life, period.

It must be said: not everyone I met in the corporate world is going to immediately combust in hell. There was some goodwill. In fact, quite a bit. Many people wished me well and wanted me to do well. Almost everybody had warm (albeit somewhat confusing) nuggets of advice. But the advice was often so cryptic to my cattle-class black ears it could have been written in codeine-induced Egyptian hieroglyphics:

- 'If your face doesn't fit, call it quits.'
- 'A spliff a day helps ease the institutional racism away.'
- 'Every negro has to be an entertainer: always keep them laughing.'
- 'Play the game.'
- 'Think like a white man, son.'

As a starting professional coming from a deeply impoverished black background I didn't know what any of the statements above meant in practice. The last two were the most baffling of all.

Play the game? Think like a white man?

What on earth did they mean? What the hell is 'the game'? On a blackness scale of one to ten, I was somewhere between Stormzy's foreskin and Phil Spector's soul – how do I 'think like white man'?

The unspeakable difficulty of being a black person, a black professional, in a white-dominated corporate environment is unique and poorly documented. For centuries, owing mainly to white supremacy-driven commercial practices and crimes (e.g. slavery, colonisation, white 'liberal' internationalism, genocide, etc.), all the associated pseudo sciences used to justify and reinforce such practices (drapetomania, phrenology, race itself as a concept, etc.) as well as the ruthless exploitation of religion and religious figures (selective Bible quotation, Christ, Richard Dawkins, neoliberalism, it's-for-their-own-good-ism, etc.), black people have worked almost exclusively with their bodies. Hence black people were, and still very much are, more likely to be found engaged in poorly remunerated and low-skilled manual labour that doesn't require much education[7] or thought. Just sheer back-breaking donkey work. Highly skilled and highly paid professional roles? Like dressage, river dancing and opioids, that is just for white folk.

Not dissimilar to big-booty white women, the black professional class is a very welcome recent phenomenon. There has long been the odd one or two here and there, but it has never been a large enough population to be described authoritatively as a 'class'. Black professionals are now truly a class and white female booty appropriators have all but wiped sisters out of a market they once almost monopolised (like the iPhone did to Nokia).[8] The problem is that, for the most part, black professionals are a class of people roaming through a mine-infested wilderness like starving wild bears with blindfolds on. A lucky few will make it to the other end of the woods, but most are likely to be blown to smithereens.

This book will help you take the blindfold off once and for all. Like a good shepherd, I, Dr Whytelaw III, the first and last word on white people, the alpha and omega of the White Man, will usher you safely through the woods. Have no fear. Walk with me.

7 In areas such as elite sport this remains the case; however, the pay is sometimes more rewarding.
8 Kim Kardashian, an off-white white woman with a fake black backside is to today what booty-free Pamela Anderson was to the 80s: the global standard of beauty.

PART 1

UNDERSTANDING THE WHITE MAN

'Racism is still with us. But it is up to us to prepare our children for what they have to meet, and, hopefully, we shall overcome.'

— Rosa Parks

CHAPTER 1

Why Think Like a White Man?

'Let us take the negro as we find him, as God designed him,
not a white man, nor the equal of a white man ...'

– Admiral Bedford Pim (1826–1886), a Royal Navy officer, Conservative MP,
Arctic explorer, barrister and author (and ardent racist)

In hundreds, if not thousands, of years from now, scholars, historians and tin-foil-hat-wearing crackpot conspiracy theorists (the latter almost certainly able to trace their lineage back to a Trump voter) will research and debate the Barack Obama phenomenon with intense fascination. I can hear the arguments now: it was his oratory, his emotional intelligence, the alarming imbecility of his predecessor or the fact that he was a man of principle and faith, which propelled him to such heights. But they will all be wrong and/or too polite to tell the unspeakable truth.

What propelled Barack Obama to prominence, his superpower, was his key talent: simply, his immense understanding of white people. Without that, he'd probably have peaked as a butler at the White House, a veteran of Ronald Reagan's war on drugs or a long-distance runner (he is, after all, 'part Kenyan' ... according to Boris Johnson).

Crucially Barack was part of the tiny, micro-fraction of black people who managed to crack the code of the most important, difficult and powerful of all white people: the White Man. Watching

Barack bob, weave and hadoken through white people, feed them sweet lies as opposed to the bitter truth, comfort their fears and soothe their tears all while maintaining the admiration of black people was beautiful to watch. When it came to the White Man, however, that brother was world class. Top five dead or alive.

He knew how to placate the White Man, how to pander to him and how to play him like a fiddle. He even knew how to put a White Man on ice. He mastered the White Man in theory, and then became the White Man's master in practice.

And if you want to go places, you have to understand white people too. Especially the White Man. It is as straightforward as that. Get your Barack on, or get barracked.

White Men, specifically those of Anglo-Saxon stock from northern Europe (who went on to steal America and other areas of the world), essentially run everything that matters on the face of the Lord God's green Earth. And whatever they don't currently run, they are actively plotting and planning to take over. Where the stakes are high enough, they are probably bombing nations (under the unbelievably effective marketing guise of 'protecting human rights') in order to do so.

White Men are the emperors, the modern pharaohs, the owners and editors of the dictionary, the purveyors and deniers of credibility and rights. And wrongs. And book deals. And, most pertinently to this book, they are more likely than anyone else to be your boss and to control, as well as define, the corporate environment or institution within which you work and hope to excel.

Fuck what you heard: corporations are not people.[1] They don't have minds of their own. The actions of corporations are not driven by nature. Or even nurture. Corporations are just entities that reflect the interests and therefore the thinking,

1 'Mitt Romney says "corporations are people"', *Washington Post*, 11 August 2011.

cultural norms and practices of their controllers and owners for the benefit of their controllers and owners.

If a corporation is controlled and owned by White Men, which is true of pretty much all major companies worldwide, then it will reflect the interests, thinking, cultural norms and practices of White Men. Which they do.

Nevertheless, in the interests of clarity, readers should be under no illusion: the proverbial White Man is not your enemy, far from it. He is much more than that: he is your owner. He owns all of us.

And I don't mean 'owner' in the Ben Affleck-ancestry[2] slave-master way – in which you could run up on him, slit his throat, crap in his birthday cake mixture or run away from him. The White Man of today has much more control over all of us than his enslaved African-owning genocidal criminal forebears.

You can't touch today's White Man. a drone will tear you limb from limb before you can even dream of getting to his throat or his cake mixture and you certainly can't run away from him. He is in your company, your algorithm, your cuisine and, most importantly, your head.

Therefore, you have to understand how he thinks and acts in order to understand how to beat him at his own game and truly experience freedom and prosperity. As the old saying goes, 'If you can't join them, study them, think like them, act like them and then obliterate them.'

Why White People?

Let's take a moment to provide a little succour to white fragility: the average white man or woman, Dave the Deplorable, the grime-quoting teacher who tried to 'save' you, or your

2 'Ben Affleck apologises for PBS slavery censorship: "I was embarrassed"', *Variety*, 21 April 2015.

perma-broke weedhead friends Will and Wendy, have little to do with the real White Man. And have little to fear from this book. In fact, they, too, stand to better themselves by reading it.

The average garden-variety white man or woman (especially if they happen to be working class – meaning broke) are, at best, on a slightly better version of the sinking ship black people have been on for a few centuries now. They, too, are sinking, just at a slower rate. They, too, need to fill up the holes and turn the ship around. This book will show them how.

Nevertheless, you cannot understand the White Man and the actions of the White Man if you don't understand 'white people'.

So, what do I mean by 'white people'?

Well, just that. I mean white people. But in the 'Africa' sense of the term. This book 'Africa-ises' white people, which means: except where absolutely necessary, it describes and chronicles white people in a manner that neither reflects nor cares for the varying complexities, diversity, difference or differences in white people. No nuance, no care, no fucks given. This book just lobs them all together in one absolutely monolithic group. You know, like white people often do with 'Africa' or 'black people'.

Some would argue, with absolute justification, that such a crass use of the term 'white people' is lacking in complexity and therefore offensive. They would probably go on to question why this book would do such a thing. Why doesn't this book just 'pander to the white woman' as the great negro writer Marlon James suggested that all writers of colour have to in order to succeed?[3] Why alienate the most powerful block of book buyers in the solar system? Was this written, produced and performed exclusively by Lauryn Hill? Does the writer hate white people?

3 'Marlon James: "Writers of colour pander to the white woman"', Sian Cain, *The Guardian*, 30 November 2015.

Good lord, no. I, and Lauryn Hill, I presume, don't harbour the least bit of disdain towards white people. In fact, I, like many a black man who makes a bit of money, love and admire white women (especially the ones who have mainstream publishing in a choke hold). I have a white wife, a white ex-wife and two white stepchildren (whom a white judge has ordered that I pay private school fees for). And, in my working life, I've found myself under more mediocre white men than Stormy Daniels. So, I clearly have the right, as well as the authority, to write about white people.

I know white people much better than they know themselves.

To be clear and ethical, I lob white people together and write about white people in a sloppy manner out of absolute laziness and an unwillingness to let facts, complexity and diversity get in the way of a potential bestseller.

The Whytelaw Classification of the Caucasian			
Type of white person	Other names	Defining qualities	Interesting fact
White Man – spelt with a capital W and M.	the Man, Da Man, White Daddy, master, massa, the boss, coloniser, enslaver, etc.	Money, absolute power, total authority, absolute impunity.	Runs the world.
White man ('white man') – spelt with a lower-case w (unless at the start of a sentence) and a lower-case m.	Lil white man, wannabe White Man, underboss, assistant to White Man, useful idiot, etc.	Some money, some power, some authority, patriarchal power. And pink skin weirdly described as white.	Often mistaken for a White Man, often mistakes himself for a White Man. Paid more than you by default.

The Whytelaw Classification of the Caucasian

Type of white person	Other names	Defining qualities	Interesting fact
White people – an all-encompassing term covering all white people. Where there is a need to differentiate, prefixes are added.	Whitey, YT, Ypipo, oyinbo, crackers, missionary, etc.	Sometimes money, and the sympathy of the police department. And pink skin weirdly described as white.	To varying degrees, they are the key secondary beneficiaries of the practices and malpractices of the White Man.
White Tragedies	(White) working-class masses, white trash, po' white trash, redneck, hillbilly, slave overseers, the police, prison wardens, etc.	Pink skin weirdly described as white only.	Easily persuaded by the White Man to believe that black people and other 'non-desirables' are the source of their brokenness.
Hollywood Villain White People (HVWP)[4]	Russians, 'Putin', Rasputin, Gopnik, Drago, Commie, Rad, etc.	Nuclear weapons. And pink skin weirdly described as white.	They're in some form of perpetual squabble with the White Man over Lord-knows-what so the White Man will buy your script if you're slandering the shit out of HVWP. Moves in silence and often outsmarts the White Man.
White people trapped in black skin	See Appendix 1.		
White Chocolate	See Appendix 1.		

4 Please note that the white man of Hollywood Villain White People descent is still a White Man. Just not at this moment or historically as *strategically* full-fat-white (i.e. anti-black) as the White Man who enslaved, colonised us and often let his mistress name and draw the borders of our countries during pillow talk. How many times in your life have you met a black person with a Russian name?

All White Men Are Not Equal

Readers will notice something extremely rare and strange for a book on the black experience: it doesn't focus exclusively on America. It draws examples, inspiration and wisdom from much further afield. Especially 'Great Britain'. And there is a reason for that …

If I had to eulogise the American White Man, forbid the precious thought, it would be a fairly swift and straightforward affair: 'Compared to his British cousin, that devil was an angel.'

And take it from a scholar, everyone in the room – the Chinese man, the Indian man, the Caribbean man, the African man, the Russian, even the freedom fries-loving French man – would give a collective 'mmm-hmmm' in complete agreement. The Irish man, his long-term whipping boy, would probably snatch the microphone and yell, 'Ah, screw yooehr weasel wahrds! Give me de bloody micrahphone, wee lad, and let me tell ya abooeht dat bastard.'

Playing with the British White Man is the very definition of playing with fire. Take the second great white war (popularly known as World War II), for example: the Germans were as tough as nails, high as Cheech and Chong[5] and, of course, 'efficient', yet they couldn't conquer the British. While the rest of Europe fell like a stripper's G-string, Britain held off against fantastic odds (with the usually uncredited help of millions of African and Asian people).

The German White Man made the Czechs choke on currywurst, romped through a drunk Poland, slapped the spliff out of the Dutch man's mouth, and reduced 'imperial' France to a

---

5 'High Hitler: how Nazi drug abuse steered the course of history', *The Guardian*, 25 September 2016.

glorified social-justice think tank, but he was forced to behave himself when it came to Britain.

Britain stood firm and alone (not really alone, but national folklore has to be upheld) against the Germans until the Americans (including 130,000 African Americans stationed in Britain) and the Russians defeated the Nazis once and for all. And we all lived happily ever after. 'We', in this instance, of course didn't include 'the blacks'. The blacks had to go home and fight the whites – both those we had just fought alongside as well as those we fought against – for our own freedom and equality. A fight we're still fighting till this day.

The British White Man is the quintessential White Man. Even the American White Man, gung-ho as he is, knows this only too well. Britain is the architect of much of the world as we know it today, thanks to its conquests and colonies. Britain played (and continues to play) a unique and interesting role in shaping the world. In fact, don't be shocked if somewhere near the very pinnacle of your firm, wherever it may be but especially in America, there is a British man. There would be no such thing as an American or a Ghanaian or a Pakistani or a Nigerian or a Saudi Arabian without Britain.

The British White Man is the White Daddy of the world. Yet, even in full knowledge of how abusive (and occasionally deadbeat) he has been, he is still loved by much of the world. Amazing. Nevertheless: while you're gazing at the British White Man romantically thinking, 'he is so lovely. He reminds me of Mr Bean and Benny Hill', he is looking at you, thinking, 'I'm so glad we reserved the right to bomb niggers.'[6]

6 According to his baby mama, this quote was made by David Lloyd George, at the time he was Leader of the Opposition. It is not clear if he was being sarcastic or serious. Nevertheless, since that statement was made Britain has been, to coin a phrase, getting its David Lloyd George on (i.e. bombing sand, land and swimming niggers).

Once upon a time, not long enough ago, the British White Man would proudly proclaim that his empire, the British Empire, was 'so vast that the sun never sets on it' – a phrase originally ascribed to the Spanish Empire, who turned out to be knock-off paella when compared to the British – which in practice means 'we had slaves toiling like fridges: nonstop.'

With that said, as years have turned to decades and decades to centuries, the British White Man has become much more sophisticated and subtle than his American counterpart. Practice has made perfect.

Case in point: unlike America, Britain never actually enslaved Africans in large numbers to toil the soil in Britain itself. Perhaps because 'the air of England is too pure for any slave to breathe' (a quote attributed to the beautiful mind of William Murray, 1st Earl of Mansfield). Britain opted instead for a more slave-from-home and 'offshore-outsourced-enslavement' approach. Popularly known as colonialism. Of course, Britain led/industrialised the great hustle of the day but they preferred to do it in 'the colonies' and the Caribbean. Entire nations such as Jamaica and Barbados were built and populated by enslaved Africans for the purpose of making Britain rich. And Britain got paid in full.

Britain's prosperity was, like that of America and many other 'developed' nations, built principally on the enslavement of Africans. Slavery was the fuel of industrialisation.

Another intriguing fact: unlike America, Britain never had segregation or any other explicit white supremacy laws on the books at home, as opposed to the slave quarters (known in sanitised terms as 'the colonies'). Yet Britain, like America, was and remains a nation deeply segregated along racial (and class) lines.

Perhaps owing in part to these superficial realities, Britain never willingly acknowledges its role in the mass enslavement and debasement of Africans. In fact, if you ask the average

British person what role Britain played in the slave trade they are likely to say that Britain ended it, which is the equivalent of a person morbidly obese as a result of over-eating standing in front of the very buffet that enhanced his waistline screaming, 'NO MORE. THIS IS NOT GOOD AND IT IS NOT GOOD FOR YOU' to other, slimmer diners. And if you dare to take it any further, don't be shocked if you're invited to 'fuck off back to Bongo-Bongo land'.

The British White Man is a top-shelf Louis Vuitton sneaker to his American cousin's bargain-bin Nike: quality over quantity. He may lead you to believe that he is a happy Manolo Ribera to America's Tony Montana but he isn't. In reality he is Alejandro Sosa to America's Tony Montana: he's the boss. Fuck with him at your peril.

To understand how the British White Man thinks is to understand how the White Man thinks, and to beat him at his own game. If you can master how to think and act like a White Man, you, too, can have an empire the sun won't set on.

CHAPTER 2

The White Man Commandments

'The only good Indian is a dead Indian.'
— General Philip H. Sheridan

'The only white man you can trust is a dead white man.'
— President Robert Gabriel Mugabe

'Can't we just all get along?'
— General Emir Osama Bin Laden[1]

Let's get deep.

Depending on who you are, where you are, and how lucky you are, the words 'white man' probably evoke imagery of a three-toothed Jerry Springer contestant clutching a Bible, a gun, his cousin's hand in marriage and a fourteen-word manifesto (possibly something along the lines of 'we must secure the existence of our people and a future for white children' or 'because the beauty of the White Aryan woman must not perish from the earth').

The key downside to such people also happens to be their biggest upside from a black professional's perspective. They're extremists and therefore easy to curtail, manipulate and, politically, castrate.

There is a gulf of difference, however, between a white man and a White Man.

1 Osama Bin Laden didn't really utter these words. Rodney King did. Both had significant squabbles with white men in uniform.

13

A White Man has the capacity or ability to direct or influence the behaviour of others or the course of events, which is, of course the definition of power. Real power. Absolute power. White Man power.

A 'conventional' white man has white skin, sometimes precious little more, and the illusion that it makes him somewhat special, important or desirable. It doesn't. It grants him some privilege, possibly vast privilege, but it doesn't for one second make him a White Man.

So, if the White Man doesn't care about a heap of English Defence League fodder, exactly what does he care about? What drives him? What does he live by? What are his values?

Thankfully, respectable scholars (principally myself) have identified the following pillars of White Man-ism, especially in the corporate space, or, as they're now known, the 'White Man Commandments'.

The White Man Commandments

1. Power is everything and winning justifies anything.

2. Politics trumps performance.

3. Compassion impedes progress.

4. Victory is only complete upon the absolute humiliation or, preferably, humiliating death of an opponent.

5. Racism has immense strategic benefit.

6. Reality is whatever a White Man (or at least a white person) says it is. Otherwise known as the 'I'm white and I say so' rule.

7. Activism is a societal ill but occasionally a useful tool.

8. Sex is a tool, a weapon and, otherwise, merely entertainment.

9. A White Man must be respected, feared or, at least, loved.

10. The White Man is God – exemplified by the beliefs that Jesus is white, Columbus discovered America, William Shakespeare is a better storyteller than Christopher Wallace, Elvis is King, the Beatles are the greatest, etc.

It is absolutely critical that you master and remember these Ten Commandments. Doing so will help you understand the motives, motivations and indeed mechanisms of the White Man and, to a much lesser extent, but by extension, quality white people (popularly known as 'the middle class'). It will also help you understand how, why and when black people adapt and adjust themselves – whether by nature or nurture – in predominantly white environments. Finally, mastering these pillars will also help you better understand and appreciate all the advice, tips and squalid suggestions I offer up to you.

As you progress through this book and, subsequently, your rise to power (i.e. career), you will notice that the values and mindset on display in the Commandments seep through much of what the White Man does, how he thinks and why he wins. And then, how you overthrow him.

187 Quick Dos and Don'ts: 1–17

1. Do cape for whiteness as if your life depends on it: your career certainly does.

2. Do follow your passion. If you're able to work on something that you're passionate about and truly love, then it will make working twenty thousand times as hard as your white peers that little bit more bearable.

3. Do demonstrate all the 'proper' emotions in a convincingly exaggerated manner and eulogise profoundly on the death of a mediocre yet widely loved (by white people) white celebrity. Or a tusk-bearing wild animal.

4. Don't wear a bow tie and a black suit if you're a man. Don't wear an all-white nun-like habit if you're a woman (it goes without saying that a niqab, hijab, burka or durag are absolutely out of the question). Anything that makes you look like a member of the Nation of Islam – or, even worse, a 'conventional non-prison Islam Muslim' – is career suicide.

5. Wear cheap non-branded glasses to interviews even if you don't need them. It softens your image and indicates a vulnerability (as opposed to blackness). Plus no one who ever wore glasses ever did anything black.

6. Do – *deep black sigh* – relax your hair or maintain an unkempt level-one cut with no partings, waves or fade. Your naptural Angela Davis afro will induce rampant perspiration, fear and spontaneous urination. Gents, embrace your Uncle Phil-style baldness; a Tupac-like clean scalp may remind white folk of Tupac.

7. Do resist the urge to quote rappers during job interviews.

8. Do be inspired by the business moves and drive of rappers. They are some of the foremost entrepreneurs and successful risk-takers of our time. Well, the ones who read their contracts before they sign them are.

9. Do keep your ethnic festivals firmly to yourself when in the office. Kwanzaa, the independence days of certain African and Caribbean nations, Jay-Z or Beyoncé's album release day, the fall of Apartheid celebrations and so on are all events which should be celebrated privately and firmly away from the eyes, ears and fears of white folk.

10. Don't wear Evisu, FUBU, Rocawear or Karl Kani on dress-down day. Tommy Hilfiger and Ralph Lauren (but certainly not US Polo Association) should be worn conservatively.

11. Do take full advantage of the coloured people time 'stereotype'. Showing up on time in black skin is occasionally enough to exceed expectations. And then get the door politely slammed in your face.

12. Don't put a picture of any of your legitimate black heroes on your desk, or on your professional or even mobile phone screensaver. No Malcolm X, no Angela Davis, no Fela Kuti, no Harriet Tubman, no Bernie Grant, no Mr Marcus, nothing. A doctored picture of you cuddling Winston Churchill or Margaret Thatcher would be wise.

13. Don't ever stray from MLK when asked who your black heroes are. Do force yourself to tear up when his 'I Have a Dream' speech is evoked for the billionth time in a blatant attempt to pacify you.

14. Don't smile or tear up when any of MLK's non-cuddly thoughts are brought up, especially things like his 'Letter from Birmingham Jail'.

15. Don't profess love or admiration for Malcolm X. In fact, condemn Malcolm for being 'too extreme for me, too negative, too divisive'. Don't forget to wash your mouth out with hot bleach afterwards.

16. Do 'perfect' your diction, i.e. sound as white and polished as possible. This is critical. Sounding remotely like a 21st-century Stepin Fetchit will damage your career irreparably. 'Speaking well', i.e. speaking like very well-to-do white people, will help your pocket swell.

17. Don't discuss politics, especially not international politics. But if you're forced to, then see to it that you are extremely anti-abortion, anti-immigration (with the exception of people from places like Sweden, Norway and, of course, Australia), anti-diversity, anti-women's rights, pro-for-profit jails, pro-prison-linked slavery, pro law 'enforcement', anti-skin beyond a certain shade of brown, PRO LEAVE (and then possibly bomb) THE EU, MAKE AMERICA GREAT AGAIN … !

CHAPTER 3

Performance + Politics = Power

'If you can convince the lowest white man he's better
than the best coloured man, he won't notice you're
picking his pocket. Hell, give him somebody to look
down on, and he'll empty his pockets for you.'

– President Lyndon B. Johnson

Let's Talk About You

It's time to get down to specifics. What is it you want to achieve?
What are your objectives in life? And by that I don't mean
the bullshit SMART[1] stuff some white man probably has you
begrudgingly doing once or twice a year. What do you *really*
want to get out of your career or your role?

Answering that question should be easier than you think.

Regardless of how you wish to frame your motivations, the
overwhelming majority of us take on professional roles for the
same reason: to accrue power and its trappings.

Don't get me wrong, a few people take up professional roles

---

1 SMART objectives: a time-wasting and painful process in which
firms require you to set annual or bi-annual objectives that are Specific,
Measurable, Achievable, Realistic and Timed (thus SMART). Largely a
box-ticking exercise, this won't help propel you; it will be used to hold
you back if not done diligently. Just do it.

for the same silly reasons people join gangs or religious sects: to look cool, be part of something special and get some degree of protection from the harsher elements of society. But sane, serious and ambitious people don't.

Whether you wish to 'help your family', 'smash the glass ceiling', 'bring hope and change to the masses', 'make a shed load of money', 'become the first black person to achieve such and such thing that white people have the opportunity to do daily', accruing power is likely to be your ultimate or underlying objective.

As a professional, you need to acquire power for yourself: no one is ever going to give it to you, and it is only through having power that you are likely to get to where you need to be to manifest your wildest and blackest dreams.

The Path to Power

So, if power is the prize, how do you go about attaining it? There are two ways to gain power in a professional setting. The first and most obvious of these is performance.

You have to be competent, especially if you are a black professional. If you're not competent, this fact will most certainly be used against you. In fact, as I'm certain you have heard, read and probably experienced, as a black professional you must be multiple times more competent than anyone else for even base recognition.[2] This is not a myth or the cries of a person with a 'chip on their shoulder'. Or the moans of some uppity black radical. It is 100% true.

Emphasis was purposefully placed on the need to be competent

2 Please see the Whytelaw Law on Black Progression for more information, p. 24.

as a black professional because, in reality, competence is not a universally required quality. Some people can get away with being flagrantly incompetent just by being very good at the other way of acquiring power: politics. Some people are able to be rubbish at both and get away with it all the way to the top.

The Infinite Potential of the Talent-free White Male

In order to attain a clear grasp of politics in action, let's go back to the 'post-racial' fantasy days of 2011 … April 2011, to be precise.

The Story of Barack and Donald

Expertise is never total, therefore every expert has their weak spot. And, as we know, Barack Obama is a master in the dark arts of understanding white people – second only to me – but he, too, had his weak spots.

Perhaps Barack wasn't familiar with the adage, 'hell hath no fury like a White Man dissed in public by a black person', or perhaps he just forgot the Ninth White Man Commandment ('A White Man must be respected, feared or, at least, loved').

In April 2011, he publicly roasted Ultra White Man Donald Trump – to his face – by obliterating the Trump-led Birther Movement,[3] simply by revealing his birth certificate.

3 A movement as blatantly racist as the British Home Office (or a Lionel Shriver article on diversity), whose members insisted that President Obama couldn't have been born in America (because, duh, he'd be in jail if he was), and eagerly scoured the earth to find evidence to support their claim that his white-as-Gwyneth-Paltrow mother squatted in some pitch-black Kenyan village and popped out lil' light-skinned Barack.

By November 2016, as the results of the election rolled in, Barack was firmly reminded: a publicly humbled White Man is a White Man on a revenge mission.

In 2011, Donald Trump was a garden-variety bloated American relic from the 80s. He was a reality-TV-show host, a serial bankrupt, Twitter troll and a dissed and dismissed joke.

Then came 30 April and he experienced something he hadn't ever had to tolerate: a black person powerful enough to put him firmly in his place.

So, what does a White Man do when he has been reduced to a racist laughing stock? Simple, he gets more racist, more vicious and runs for president.

As far as party and presidential politics were concerned, Trump was:

- *Irredeemably inexperienced;*
- *Irredeemably tainted;*
- *Irredeemably unsuitable;*
- *Irredeemably irredeemable.*

Donald Trump was one of, if not the very worst, candidate ever to run for anything, anywhere. Yet, of course, he won. And won decisively. (Men like Donald Trump do become president in, say, African nations but they're never ever elected. Africans are far too smart to vote for guys like Donald Trump.)

Yes, he was, and still is, a heady cocktail of -isms, phobias and testosterone, but he knew his customer exceptionally well. So, he decided to feed his customer their drug of choice, which just so happened to be the most addictive of all drugs: white supremacy. Good old-fashioned George Wallace-style racism.

Screw the fact that he was as compromised as an American businessman-turned-politician caught on tape drenched in a

Moscow prostitute's urine: he knew that after eight years of stable, prosperous and scandal-free negro rule,[4] *white people needed some good ol' southern-fried racism. So he made it clear that the racist they needed was him. And lo, white people put him in the White House.*

Politics

This is where things get tricky. Organisations will train you on your role, assist with performance, and you can, in good faith, ask other people when you get confused. Playing politics, however – whether at country or company level – is a filthy game (even when family values-spouting Tory politicians are not involved). It is the most difficult part of professionalism; there is no training for it. In fact, no one can really explain to you what it is or even if it exists. You will just find yourself in the middle of it and having to deal with it. And you'll know you're in the middle of it when you're up in the middle of the night crying into a bucket of ice cream.

To ask someone about politics in the workplace is to admit to political weakness or naïvety, which will eventually be exploited.

So, if you need to be politically savvy in order to excel as a professional, what do you do in practice? The answer is paradoxically simple yet complex. You need to treat every working day with the shrewdness and forced optimism of a desperate political campaign. Metaphorically kiss some babies, hug the bigot, 'reject and denounce' Louis Farrakhan's support,[5] form

4 This assumes that you don't consider the black Africans getting enslaved and lynched in Obama/Cameron/Sarkozy-liberated Libya to be a scandal.
5 'Obama denounces Farrakhan endorsement', *Wall Street Journal*, 26 February 2016 and 'Dems denounce Farrakhan rhetoric amid pressure from GOP', *Politico*, 8 March 2018.

alliances with strange bedfellows, change your accent if need be (like Hillary Clinton or Maggie Thatcher), show those pearly whites ... Do whatever it takes.

Politically speaking: you need to make everyone 'go black'. For you at least. And, hopefully, like a Kardashian, never go back.

You want them, white people, to be thinking Nat King Cole when they see you. Not Nat Turner. To think pre-financial crisis Gordon Brown and not Bobby, Chris or Orlando Brown. Pound sterling and not Raheem Sterling. The more white people love you, the easier and more prosperous your career will be. The more power you amass, the more cash you will stash.

Either master the politics and acquire the power you crave or be prepared to shine shoes for a long time to come. It's a straight choice: play the game, or be played.

In all organisations there is a balance between politics and performance. Some organisations are near total political jungles, others only suffer a small dose of politics; but there's no workplace where politics is entirely absent.

Power is the prize. Performance gets you in the game but it is politics that keeps you in the game and eventually gets you on the podium.

The Whytelaw Law on Black Progression

Here is the Whytelaw formula for calculating how far and how fast a black person will proceed in any given corporation.

$$(2Y \times Performance) + Politics^X = Black\ progression\ (Hpy)$$

Formula explained:

Y depicts how many times harder black people have to work than white people. Pegged at one, as we know that the efforts of black people are never ever held in greater esteem than the efforts of white people. It's multiplied by two as it is scientifically proven that black people have to work at least twice as hard.

Performance means level of effort plus ability to act upper middle-class white. This ensures we don't give the White Man the impression that we don't believe in the concept of taking some responsibility for one's own situation.

Politics is self-explanatory.

X is the level of white supremacist intensity within the organisation.

Hpy – Hillbillies per year is the official measure of black progress within an organisation. It means that named organisation is an environment in which the average black person will progress at the speed it takes the identified number of the lowest quality possible of white person. 100 hillbillies = 1 White Man.

Example:

10Hpy means that it will take the average black person the amount of time it would take ten Jeremy Kyle contestants, collectively, to attain a promotion, a pay rise and, ultimately, a little power. Which also means that the average black person is progressing at 10% of the speed of the average White Man.

IF YOU'RE STRUGGLING TO UNDERSTAND THIS FORMULA, JUST THINK YOU HAVE TO WORK AT LEAST TWICE AS HARD TO GET HALF AS MUCH.

CHAPTER 4

Compassion or Progression? Decision Time

'In my experience, the African people are immensely forgiving. They have forgiven the indignities that they suffered in recent times. To encourage the kind of attitude of fervent desire for reparation suggested here would go against the grain, certainly among Africans, because it is not in their nature.' [1]

– Lucius Cary, 15th Viscount Falkland (1996)

'**G**ood guys finish last', 'the good die young', 'the good pay for the meals but never close the deals'. Why? Because the good are full of compassion. Anyone trying to get higher up the food chain has to let their compassion slide and embrace moral ambiguity. At least on a temporary basis.

If there is one thing black people are better endowed with than anyone else (remove your head from the sewer of stereotype), it is compassion – and its cousins empathy,

1 See: http://www.publications.parliament.uk/pa/ld199596/ldhansrd/vo960314/text/60314-26.htm.

sympathy, kindness, concern, consideration and benevolence. 'I-forgives-him-lawd-ism'.

The White Man called it correctly: black people are especially giving and forgiving ... to just about everyone (with the notable occasional exception of each other).

I learned early on that, for me as a black professional, in order to rise through the ranks and really attain power, I had to leave that legendary, world-renowned, all-too-profitable (for others), very black brand of compassion at home. And I needed to adopt the most ruthless of mindsets possible: the mindset of the White Man who would tear your cheek from your face before he even considered turning his one first.

In order to get to the top (the real top, the White Man top), you have to exhibit a degree of cut-throat determination (which may figuratively, and sometimes even literally, necessitate the cutting of a few throats – although let's be clear, this book does not advocate murder or attempted murder, not even manslaughter). Every collective ever to taste greatness and every group of people ever to rise to power have one thing in common: they are a pack of absolute bastards, with a long trail of victims ready to attest to this fact. And the reason for this is that compassion is the mortal enemy of progression.

Ask the Scots about the English, the Poles about the Germans and the Native Americans about the pilgrims. Ask the black South Africans about the white South Africans, the Gazelles about the Lions. Ask the Chinese about the Japanese, the Vietnamese about the Chinese. Ask the African Americans about the European Americans. Go and ask Africans about the Europeans (and the Arabs). And, as we have already noted, ask just about everyone about the British.

The history of human prosperity and progression is a history of the merciless exploitation of one person or people by another. Where there is great prosperity there is usually compassion-free flagrant atrocity and a really great public relations officer working overtime to gently perfume away the stench of shit.

Compassion is out of the question and out of the window. There is no alternative model.

Appearance Is Everything

Even though you are aiming to be a compassion-free morally bankrupt opportunist, you still need to exude the appearance of compassion.

You don't get to David Cameron (beneficiary of slavers),[2] Nicholas Sarkozy (beneficiary of dictators)[3] and Silvio Berlusconi (benefactor of underage 'prostitutes')[4] levels of extreme success and power with a heart or head full of compassion for others. You get to that level by being able to create the *impression* that you have a head and heart full of compassion for others. You get to that level by doing what you have to do for you, no matter the cost to others. The trick is making it feel like you're doing it *for* them, even when you're often doing it *to* them.

The perfect example of faux compassion is the British Empire. Why do people still want to align themselves with it today given its history of clear brutality? Three reasons:

- White supremacist brutality never prevails, because when it does it's not called white supremacist brutality. It is called

2 'How do we know David Cameron has slave owners in family background?', *The Guardian*, 29 September 2015.
3 'Sarkozy charged over Libyan cash for campaign', *Daily Telegraph*, 21 March 2018.
4 'Berlusconi found guilty after case that cast spotlight on murky premiership', *The Guardian*, 24 June 2013.

'you should be grateful we taught your kind to speak English'.

- The British Empire was much better at long-term public relations as a result of the fact that they became the global establishment.

- In the scorching true words of the late great moderate white of words, George Orwell: 'niggers don't count'.[5]

No matter what shenanigans and criminality it may have embarked on, Britain has always cloaked itself (and marketed itself) in the translucent cloth of philanthropy and humanitarianism, prospectively and retrospectively (even if that means destroying all evidence to the contrary).[6] If you speak to the average Briton today, regardless of skin tone – vanilla, ox red strawberry ice cream, redbone, café au lait, mocha or even Nero Milano hot chocolate – they will often tell you that Britain only did great things in, say, Africa. What is even more bizarre is that Africans themselves bestow honours on Britain for their own subjugation and debasement.[7]

Like America in Iraq and Afghanistan, Russia in Crimea and Syria, and any number of white women in marriages with black football players, Britain was, of course, in Africa to do well as opposed to do good. But the genius of Britain is that it managed

5 'Not Counting Niggers', George Orwell, 1939: http://orwell.ru/library/articles/niggers/english/e_ncn.

6 'Britain destroyed records of colonial crimes', *The Guardian*, 18 April 2012.

7 In 2014, while celebrating the hundredth anniversary of Britain's forced amalgamation of Nigeria, the then Nigerian president, Goodluck Jonathan, bestowed an honour on the man who completed the amalgamation and tasked his lady partner with finding a name for the newly formed country: Lord Frederick Luggard. Luggard was himself described by the Conservative Mayor of London as a 'savage kill-the-natives type' (*The Churchill Factor: How One Man Made History*, Boris Johnson, 2014).

to convince both itself and its victims, the coloniser and the colonised, that it was a heroic and benevolent 'world power', i.e. White Daddy.

If this proves anything, it proves that public relations matter. You have to manage and manipulate your image and the overall narrative. You have to make people love you, even as you're robbing, killing and castrating them. Always make them think that even when you're being a bastard it's for their own good.

This was true of Empire, it is true of the corporate empire, it's true of exploitative white women,[8] and it is true of you if you want to go places. You may be a bastard. But you must look, feel and sound as lovable as Ronald McDonald ... even though in reality you are little more than an artery-clogging corporate whore.

Victimhood

Victimhood:

- Perhaps the only 'hood' the White Man doesn't want to see you in.
- The only 'hood' white people will never gentrify.
- One of the enduring pet hates of white people when it comes to black people.

'How bloody dare this uppity negro have the sheer audacity to feel like a victim just because I missold her a sub-prime

---

8 'Emmanuel Eboue lifts the lid on bitter divorce battle that left him with nothing and how he hasn't seen his three kids since June', *Daily Mirror*, 24 December 2017.

mortgage, plunged her into financial ruin[9] and then deported her to Jamaica "in error"?'[10]

No matter what life (i.e. white people) may have thrown at you and, no doubt, what it will throw at you, you better not feel sorry for yourself. You better not feel like a victim. Don't worry. Be merry. Or else.

Sadly, to avoid becoming a victim, you have to be ready to make victims of others, kind of like a prison bully in the shower. And making victims of others is where things get even trickier.

Black people have no problem making victims of each other. It is the basis of the multi-billion-dollar gangsta rap industry as well as the private prisons industry (two industries which may or may not have a reciprocal relationship).

Black-on-black one upmanship is as simple as eating hot chocolate cake in the middle of a break-up or evoking 'black-on-black crime' on *Fox News*. When black people are required to perform the same squalid manoeuvres in white spaces against white people? We're quick to back down.

There are many reasons for this, but here is a critical one: there is a value associated with white people that just isn't associated with black people. Whites rule everything around you. No one wants to bite the hand that has the potential to choke you. And that represents a clear psychological disadvantage for the black professional – one that must be levelled in order for the black professional to truly reach their potential.

9 'Bank accused of pushing mortgage deals on blacks', *The New York Times*, 6 June 2009.
10 'Windrush: More than just coincidental errors', *BBC News*, 17 April 2018.

Levelling the Psychological Playing Field

A great modern way a black professional can level the psychological playing field when in head-to-head opposition with white professionals is to listen to hip-hop. Not any old hip-hop. Certainly, no fluffy teddy bear Mos Def and Talib Kweli or Best of Will Smith shit. Nope, you need the most violent, degrading and shocking hip-hop you can find. Hip-hop that sounds like Willie Lynch conceived it, Joseph Goebbels wrote it, George Bush Snr produced and Apartheid-Nazi-Rhodesia-Breitbart Records distributed it.

It's quite easy to find it too: turn on the radio.

The black professional just needs to make one simple change to these rap records: when your favourite rapper evokes imagery of inflicting some degree of unbelievable savagery which will inevitably be against black people (other than the rare occasion a rapper gets into it with Eminem), replace that imagery in your mind with a white person. Repeat this as often as possible. A few entry-level suggestions:

- For those passive aggressive 'hints' (perhaps about your timekeeping), Stormzy's 'Shut up' should do the trick.
- For appraisals, throw on 'Hold Me Back' by Rick Ross.
- For 'quick chats' when you suspect it's bad news: ask for five minutes to pop into the loo and throw on 'Bad News' by G Unit.
- When you're scheduled for a redundancy-risk discussion you may want to throw on 'Pray' by MC Hammer.
- If you're feeling a little too lazy to change the lyrics, then pop on '100 Years' by Plies.

Alternative Method of Levelling the Psychological Playing Field

If you find altering hip-hop lyrics to be a little demanding, there is another equally effective method of levelling the playing field: it's called switching on the news (or social media) and witnessing the latest white-on-black outrageousness. And let what white people are capable of sink into your soul.

In conclusion, you have to decide: compassion or progression? Victimhood or victory? Rags or riches? Success or sympathy? You or them?

187 Quick Dos and Don'ts: 18–34

18. Do arm yourself with one of these names for when you're asked who you foremost admire: Ronald Reagan, Margaret Thatcher, Winston Churchill and Thomas Jefferson (but under no circumstances reveal that the latter is your great-great-great-great-great grandfather). If you must veer into the ethnic, straight choice: Mandela, MLK or Jesus Hussain Christ.

19. Don't ever return a bust of Winston Churchill (in the event that you somehow manage to find one on your desk) or describe Churchill as anything less than an absolute hero. Even if he tortured your grandfather.

20. Don't mistake the office party for a house party or a BBQ. Dance, but not too well. A Barack-on-Ellen-style frail-white-grandmother shuffle should suffice, a Michelle-on-Ellen-style 'Tip Drill'-video-worthy throw-down will ruin you.

21. Do order salad when at a business meal. Even if you – like most black people – hate the taste. It makes it seem as if you value your health and your life, therefore smashing multiple major black stereotypes with one tasteless leafy plate.

22. Don't order two main courses (perhaps one as a starter and one as a main) because it would be 'cost-effective' when at a business meal.

23. Do master the names of at least three different types of fantastically expensive (and therefore) 'sophisticated' cheeses.

24. Do order cheese for dessert when at a business meal.

25. Don't delude yourself: you know good and well that 'cheese-cake' does not qualify as a type of cheese.

26. Do keep the fact that your parents were Panthers or Freedom Riders or were in the Mau Mau or Brixton Uprisings firmly to yourself. Despite feeling incredibly proud of them.

27. Do mention that your cousin's girlfriend's babysitter's hair-dresser's cousin on her mother's side fought in the Gulf War, Vietnam, Iraq, Libya or any other pointless, counter-produc-tive and probably illegal war that white people approved of.

28. Do seize any opportunity to pay white people the supreme ultimate compliment: 'You've lost weight.' Even if they have done the opposite.

29. Don't wear 'loud' jewellery – 'loud' in this context meaning black. You'll be maliciously mistaken for a rapper, a gangsta or a benefits 'cheat' (otherwise known as a direct repa-ration seeker). No more than one ring on your fingers, preferably on your wedding finger, no multiple finger rings, small earrings (but only if you're a woman), no company logo medallions, no Tupac-style nose rings and certainly no 80s crack peddler-style chains. Don't let Afropunk or *Hidden Colors* get you fucked up: no bone in your nose either.

30. Do wear a ring on your wedding finger when going for inter-views and while you're still on probation (i.e. job probation – not jail). Even if you're hopelessly single – in fact, especially if you're hopelessly single. It signifies commitment, maturity, stability and desperation.

31. Don't sign off a professional email or phone call with the words 'God bless'. In fact, don't ever evoke God in a professional setting. Except in the context of 'God save the Queen' or 'In God we trust' or 'God damn, we stand to make a lot of money if we do such and such.' But never in the context of 'God rain down fire and keep these crackers off my back' and, forbid the dreaded thought, 'God is great' – especially not in Arabic.

32. Do happily split the bill equally when you go out for group drinks or dinner, professional or otherwise. The few peppercorns you'll save by ticking off the items you consumed on the receipt will lose you a fortune in missed opportunities as a result of looking cheap and socially inept.

33. Don't be shocked when white people use other white people as a means of creating a picture of 'diversity' within your firm that just doesn't exist. For example, a straight white Englishman in New York may be held up as a poster child for the firm's commitment to ethnic diversity.

34. Do place a picture of extremely light-skinned children on your desk. Doesn't matter who they belong to. Just allow people to assume they belong to you. This will hopefully garner sympathy when it is time for budget cuts. It's the photographic equivalent of saying 'please don't shoot! There is a white person in my life and we have procreated together!'

CHAPTER 5

Shock and Awe

'What we realise is that white comfort is more
important than black lives ...'

– Alisyn Camerota, CNN anchor, 30 May 2018

Negroes know the drill with horror movies. The token negro character, by some turn of comedic misfortune or fate, always finds themselves killed first[1] or, on a good pay day for the actor, being reserved for a uniquely savage and protracted murder later down the line.

In the laughably poor 2007 film *The Hills Have Eyes II*, Missy, the obligatory token 'black' character, played by Daniella Alonso, who actually happens to be Puerto Rican, Peruvian and Japanese (a token black person couldn't even get the role of the token black person), surprisingly lingered on. I initially thought it was a deliberate and commendable attempt to diversify the horror genre. Perhaps Missy was on a horror diversity scheme of sorts?

Then what was really going on was revealed in the last act: Missy was savagely raped by the antagonist monster. In the cinema where I saw the film, people were laughing out loud at this absurd scene. I couldn't laugh. I identified with her pain, metaphorically.

1 *Scream II, Ghost Ship, Day of the Dead, One Missed Call, The Unborn*, etc.

I hate to be the bearer of racist news, but you *are* that character. You are Missy. No prizes for guessing who the monster is.

The treatment of black professionals at the hands of many a corporation is not entirely different to how black people are treated in horror films: horrendously and with only slightly less lethal results (if you're lucky).

So, the first thing any black professional should prepare for is shock. You will, without a shadow of a doubt, be subjected to things that you will consider shocking and outrageous. Some of it will be accidental; some of it will be on purpose. How you react will be watched and remembered.

If positive or passive, your reaction could be the making of you. If hostile, in kind, or what would be deemed disproportionate (i.e. 'too black'), it will almost certainly break you.

Quickly developing a shock absorption mechanism, or at least creating the appearance of having one, is critical to your professional progression, because to lose your temper (although often a natural, just and understandable reaction) could be professionally fatal.

In-depth analysis: one of the key tightropes that any black professional must walk is that of avoiding tags. Especially racially loaded negative labels and stereotypes; those terms that may not be racist on the face of it but, in reality, everyone knows are as racist as Slave Bibles.[2]

Think 'angry', 'attitude', 'intimidating', 'aggressive', 'thuggish', 'emotional', 'threatening', 'drama queen', 'rude-boy', 'Kenyan', 'Muslim'. These are patent career-killing labels, racial dog whistles that are often permanently ascribed to (black) people who momentarily lose their temper or react negatively

2 Which, it should be noted, were created in London ... a year after the Act of Parliament that supposedly abolished the slave trade. See: 'The shocking "Slave Bible": Here are the parts that were deleted to manipulate slaves', *CBN News*, 18 February 2018.

to aggravation. Losing a black credit profile[3] is a lot easier than losing those tags.

Imagine this scenario: you're deeply insulted by a (white) colleague during a work-related exchange. Perhaps things quickly escalate from a mild disagreement on the PowerPoint positioning of a graph to her big bad white self suddenly hitting you with a deeply anti-black insult: she calls you a 'disgusting greasy nappy-headed nigger'. She sprints to senior management and – swiftly ensuring the first draft of history favours her – lies about you. She falsely accuses you of insulting her, rather than the other way around. In the process, she unleashes one of the most potent weapons white women possess: white motherfucking tears.

Jesus walk with you.

With white tears detonated and without asking for your side of the story, excited and over-cautious management takes the bait and escalates the issue to the most despised group in corporate life: Human Resources (aka Human Remains, aka Hood Rats, aka the Aiding & Abetting Department, aka the Why Is There A White Man At The Top Of This All-Female Department? department).

HR hears about the white tears and bursts into a frenzy of panic. They immediately launch an investigation, without even informing you of the complaint. But, as you're a shrewd networker, you're tipped off to what's going on. In short, like Tiger Woods, after it was discovered that his white-women-itis was significantly worse than originally thought, you're a black person in a predominantly white space in very deep trouble.

There's no doubt that this is shocking behaviour by the

3 'Credit scores in America perpetuate racial injustice. Here's how', *The Guardian*, 13 October 2015.

company. You go home every night for a few days knowing that you're unjustly in trouble and your job (or career even), livelihood and good name are at risk.

Then the ancestors come to your rescue. Facts emerge. Multiple (white) people who saw the entire fiasco play out make it clear that you are the victim here and not the villain. Ashe!

At this point, you will feel vindicated, and after vindication comes righteous indignation; after righteous indignation comes 'Eye Of The Tiger' fighting spirit, and then comes making it abundantly bloody clear that they're a pack of incompetent clowns who tried to screw you over and you're NOT HAVING IT.

You're laying down the law once and for all and making it clear that this had better not happen again. And you want everyone to know in painfully humbling detail how and why they were wrong. And to get down on their knees and apologise.

In the 'real world' (i.e. imaginary utopian world) where all is equal, fair, lovely (and free from whiteness), you would be right to do so. In fact, it is arguably your right to do so. However, doing so in a professional setting, as a black person, would be a costly mistake.

Your objective is to acquire power for yourself and move up the ladder. Alienating the existing power structure or rallying them against you as a result of an actual or perceived injustice won't help your cause. Whether they're right or wrong is immaterial. What matters is that they are powerful.

In reality, in this scenario you only have three options:

1. Take on the power structure and topple them completely. Ensure they lose their jobs (or at least their power) and ensure you acquire their power for yourself. If you fail, they will certainly be coming for that ass.

2. Absorb the shock and move on. Clear your name, but do everything possible not to aggravate the situation further. This could serve to further ingratiate you, i.e. help you acquire power for yourself. However, make sure you keep a record – written and oral – of what happened. Yes, it's the equivalent of wearing a wire, but you never know when this might become useful in the future.

3. Consult a legal professional for expert advice and make them, the company, pay (financially) for the distress caused to you. Given the risk of potential reputational damage to the firm as a result of you suing, they may want to pay you to fuck off. But if they don't, then tread carefully. This could quickly spiral out of your control.

A working relationship is just that: a relationship. In order for it to work, sometimes you will have to create the impression that all is forgiven and forgotten.[4] Sometimes you're going to go through a bitter divorce and move on. And other times you're going to have to go all Lisa 'Left Eye' Lopez[5] or Elin Nordegren[6] up in there.

Whatever you do, you must think with your head and not your heart: keep your eye on the prize.

Barack Obama, the quintessential black professional, is a

4 Forgiveness should be viewed in a similar light to cancer or the police: irredeemably bad. Do not ever truly forgive and forget anything in a professional setting. Wait for the right time to bring it up and use it against your enemies.
5 'Left Eye burns down boyfriend Andre Rison's house', complex.com, 12 July 2011.
6 'Tiger Woods "had plastic surgery after wife battered him with a nine-iron", claims leading American sportswriter', *Daily Mail*, 30 December 2009.

perfect example of a black professional retaining their cool in the face of shock (and awe). Whenever he was debating opponents, whether Hillary Clinton, John McCain or Mitt Romney (or even Bobby Rush, the former Black Panther who handed Obama his own backside in the 2000 Illinois congressional race), or having what turned out to be highly expensive playground tiffs with the likes of Donald Trump, his opponents could all demonstrate a degree of assertiveness that Obama simply could not. For him to respond to their combativeness in a similar manner would see him labelled 'angry', 'aggressive' or 'thuggish'. Or 'Muslim'. It would have been a campaign killer. A career killer. An aggressive form of exclusively antiblack cancer.

So, Obama had to stay above the fray. Difficult, without question, but it had its benefits: it made him look more professional, more stable, more capable and, ultimately, more presidential than his opposition.

The Subservience Test

Let's go back. Way back. Back to when I believed in the fairy tale of 'equal opportunities'. Back to my first pay review day.

The Story of Boulé's Subservience Test

Pay review day: the only day of the year that really matters. The office is as excited as a Klansman at a Trump rally (or vice versa). Same shit, different toilet. Pay review day or not, a black person in the white corporate world remains a black person in the white corporate world, so naturally I had to wait for everyone else to find out their figures first and watch in awe as they did the Floss.[7] I mean, come on, what did you think? A black person would be prioritised? This isn't jail sentencing.

But at least this meant that by the time my ten minutes in an airless room rolled around I had heard enough about other comparable colleagues' figures that it felt safe to expect a bonus of at least five figures. Fair enough, they were all talcum powder-complexioned and I am as black as the bottom of a pot of Jollof, but my rating for the year was up there with the highest of performers amongst them.

And this was, after all, an 'equal opportunities' employer.

So, when my boss James 'Jim' Crowther (let's call him 'Jim Crow' for subtlety purposes) warmly shook my hand and congratulated me for a good year before telling me that I'd be getting a bonus of £2,000 (roughly a tenth of what my (white) colleagues were getting), I was as stunned as the police racial equality adviser who got tasered by the very police force he was advising.[8] Nevertheless, I got my Oliver Twist on and asked for more.

A few days later, during a working lunch, Jim waltzed right out of the racist closet and asked me to fetch him a glass of water. Something he would never dare ask a white person (well, perhaps an intern or a messenger – he is an asshole after all). I laughed at his 'joke' and told him to go fetch his own water. He obliged. Upon sitting down he

7 An enduring white tribal dance. The only dance white people managed to invent in the timeframe black people invented the running man, the twerk, the milly rock, the moonwalk, the doo wop, the shmurda, the locomotive, the twist, the whip nae nae, the skanky leg, the tootsie roll, the bop, the butterfly, the crank dat, the dab, the hotline bling, etc, etc … black creative genius … etc, etc.

8 'Police sergeant who tasered her force's own race relations adviser found not guilty of assault', *The Independent*, 18 May 2018.

whispered in my ear: 'remember that pay rise you wanted? Dream on.'

Weeks later, back in the airless room, Jim calmly explained that 'the books are closed and there is nothing we can do on the bonus front, I'm afraid. Keep working hard and we'll take care of you next year.'

Two months later he made me redundant. While I was on holiday.

A few years later – new company, I was much more senior, but somehow someway: same shit. Something similar happened. Only this time the item on demand was a sandwich with a 'healthy dose of cheese and tomato'. Scarred by the experience, I complied with the request. My soul gradually evaporated as the pennies for the sandwich fell into my hand.

This was modern racism at its most potent: damaging to the victim's prospects, very bold and near impossible to prove. I'd much rather have been called 'the coolest monkey in the jungle'[9] and had bananas thrown at me.

So, what can we learn from this?

As months flew by I managed to let go of enough shame to speak to a learned friend about the matter. She explained that it was probably 'just' a subservience test – a means of ensuring that you're a team player and are willing to get your hands dirty if needed.

As the years have passed I've cracked the code: she was only half right. It was indeed a subservience test, but it was not a means of ensuring that I was a team player. That was already evident. And so, the test should have been pointless.

---

9 'H&M apologises for image of black child wearing "coolest monkey in the jungle" hoodie', *Daily Telegraph*, 9 January 2018.

THINK LIKE A WHITE MAN

But if not to ascertain my credentials as a 'team player' then what was its purpose?

Ponder the following:

- Other than the fact that he was a horny old man, why did President Bill Clinton ask his twenty-three-year-old intern, Monica Lewinsky, to 'moisten' his cigar? (There should be no need to explain this to anyone who went through puberty in the mid to late 90s.)

- Other than the fact that he may have been hungry, why did Puff Daddy make a music group he was forming on a reality TV show march for miles on foot to go and buy him a slice of cheesecake only for him to have left by the time they returned?

- Other than the fact that the club may be running a racist entry policy, why does the nightclub bouncer consider your shoes unsuitable for his club even though they just let in someone else sporting the same footwear?

- Other than the fact that they absorbed dictatorial tendencies from the old country, why do African parents ask their children to fly across oceans in a hurry to fetch them a remote control only half a metre in front of them?

The answer to all of the above is one and the same: because they can, because they have the power to do so.

People with power often feel the need to demonstrate that they have it. Sometimes they do this to do good, other times to do well, and, sadly, more often than not, just to make themselves feel better.

The purpose of the subservience test is to make the powerful feel good about being, well, powerful. And, perhaps even to help the powerful ascertain an understanding of who is happy to be under their heel.

Of course, if you 'fail' the subservience test and show that you have a little Toussaint Louverture blood flowing through your veins, then you can expect to be crushed. Quickly. Which is exactly what Jim Crow did to me.

For a black person, the natural racism that comes as part and parcel of the subservience test is a terrible conundrum. Do you submit (like the Saudis) or resist (like Saddam)? Do you accept temporary degradation in order to move forward in the long term? Do you move that ass to the back of the bus in order to get to your destination? Or do you blow the bus up?

My advice: take one for the team. Comply with the request. Treat it like a police stop-and-search session. (As the great Khalid Abdul Muhammad advised, during a stop-and-search request you are behind enemy lines: name, rank, serial number, a silent prayer for survival and, above all, shut up.) But keep a record of this treatment in case you need to bring it up at some point. Swallow your pride, prepare for shame and embarrassment, demonstrate the requisite subservience and just do it.

It's a small price to pay for power. And always remember: power is the prize. Once you get it – and you will – the people who made you subservient will fetch glasses of water and sand-wiches for you. Why? Because you will make them.

If they don't bow before you, their dead bodies will float by as you sit by the banks of the river enjoying a cold bottle of Supermalt. Metaphorically, of course.

Shock, insults, lies, subservience tests: none of these are con-clusively race issues on the face of it. For that, you should be thankful. For if they do become a race or racism issue, even if you're the clear victim, it's very bad news. For you.

187 Quick Dos and Don'ts: 35–51

35. Don't bleach your skin. There is no recorded case in human history of skin bleaching having a long-term positive impact on a black person's career prospects. It's a waste of time, money and, quite possibly, life. BUT do bleach your teeth and let those pearly whites show. Tyrese's entire career is testimony to the power of this.

36. Do 'bleach' your name if it doesn't sound white enough. Born 'Mohamed Muktar Jama Farrakhan from Somalia'? Refashion yourself as 'Mo Farah from the sweet city of San Francisco'. Georgios Kyriacos Panayiotou? Change that shit to 'George Michael' (or open a kebab shop). 'Raven', 'Beyoncé', 'Barack Hussain Obama'? You'll never go platinum with names like those.

37. Do publicly lavish praise on the works of Clint Eastwood, Ridley Scott and D. W. Griffith.

38. Don't ever mention your love of the works of Spike Lee, Amma Asante, Steve McQueen, Ava DuVernay, Bola Agbaje and Destiny Ekaragha, the Hughes Brothers or John Singleton.

39. Do publicly disparage the works of Tyler Perry and Noel Clarke. Uppity professional blacks and bigoted whites alike will both love you for this. Win-win. But do quietly ensure that you learn from Tyler's and Noel's business moves.

40. Do familiarise yourself with at least three different types of fantastically expensive wines. Being able to spurt out the French name given to an overpriced bunch of rotten grapes – while black – will blow white minds.

41. Don't delude yourself, you know very well that Alizé, Hennessy and Nigerian Guinness are not expensive fine wines.

42. Do note the following polite long-hand terms for 'Nigger, we're not hiring niggers.':

- 'I just don't think you would fit in …'
- 'Yes, I totally understand you're the first (and probably the last) person to go to university in your family and you grew up eating sand on the worst estate in the nation … but class is the issue for us right now.'
- 'You're … overqualified/underqualified/extra medium qualified.'
- 'Look, the Obama era was fun while it lasted but we must go back to normal now …'
- 'It's diversity of thought that really matters.'

43. Don't pick a rap song when you go for the company karaoke evening. If one is forced upon you, ensure that you demonstrate sub Iggy Azalea rapping skills when performing it.

44. Do remember where you are when the accidentally booked DJ throws on 'Back That Ass Up' at the office party and the 'liberal' in the office feels the need to demonstrate her 'love of diversity' by dragging you to your feet for a risqué waltz. The office party shouldn't ever be mistaken for '88 Freaknik in Atlanta, the Notting Hill Carnival or the 2018 Presidents Club Dinner.

45. Don't 'twerk somethin'', 'kick a little freestyle' or 'belt out a negro spiritual' for senior management at the office party.

46. Don't angrily respond 'No, I am not some form of fucking domesticated exotic animal' when someone asks if they can touch your hair for the umpteenth time.

47. Don't ever reveal that Michael Jackson easily surpassed Elvis and the Beatles both creatively and commercially. It is a fact that white people just cannot handle.

48. Do profess love and admiration for Elvis Presley and Paul McCartney and lavish praise on their work … even though

Elvis fucked over more black people than a credit ratings agency and McCartney ruined every single track by a black artist that he appeared on.

49. Do agree that Robin Williams was a better and more original comic than Eddie Murphy, Richard Pryor or Paul Mooney. Even though he wasn't and the latter two gave him his break.

50. Don't publicly congregate with more than five black people at any one time unless there are at least ten white people present for each black person.

51. Do try not to respond 'Isaiah Washington or OJ Simpson or Mo'Nique or Meghan Markle' (or any other black actors that white people don't like but can't *quite* put their finger on why) when asked who you would like to play you in your biopic.

CHAPTER 6

See No Racism, Hear No Racism, Speak No Racism

Interviewer: 'How do we stop racism?
Morgan Freeman: 'Stop talking about it.'

'You're an embarrassment to me. You look like a fucking bitch in heat, and if you get raped by a pack of niggers, it will be your fault.'

– Mel Gibson, director of *The Passion of the Christ*
(in discussion with his wife)

The Story of Tyrone

'Come in, Tyrone. Take a seat,' says Sharon from Human Resources with a beautiful smile fixed in her David Coulthard-esque jaw. 'How are yooooouu? It's so good to see you!'

'Sharon, it's great to see you too. I am very well, thanks,' replies Tyrone.

'Splendid. Thank you so much for your time today,' says Sharon with a well-rehearsed look of deep white sincerity on her face.

'Tracey is only here to take notes for this meeting.' Sharon signals to her personal assistant.

'Let me know if I'm speaking too fast and I'll slooooow it dooooown,' jokes Tyrone. Tracey smiles in response and then returns to chewing her pen.

'Right. Time for business. As you know, we're here today to discuss your recent expression of dissatisfaction with your career prospects within your department. Specifically, you have expressed frustration at what you consider to be a lack of progress in the forms of increased pay and promotion. Have I read this correctly?' she asks.

'That is correct. I've been the highest-grossing sales person for the last four years, I have retained all of my clients, and many of my ideas have been acknowledged as ground-breaking for our industry. I cannot see what more I could do in order to be promoted.

'In the same period, I have seen other people who have contributed a fraction of my efforts promoted above me. I'm afraid I'm left with no option but to state my concerns.'

By this stage Tyrone is sounding a little bit nervous.

'I see,' says Sharon. 'Why do you think this, erm, perceived ... discrepancy exists?'

'I am not entirely certain what is driving this or why this is happening, but—'

Sharon politely interrupts, and, leaning in to demonstrate compassion[1] and says, 'Tyrone, this conversation is completely off the record.[2] So, you can be honest with

1 Faux compassion is easily mistakable for real compassion. The key difference in sorting one from the other is the motivation of the person providing it. Mistaking the professional motherly care of Human Resources for the care of a friend is the definition of stupidity.
2 Do not ever believe those words. Everything is on the record when it comes to black people in white spaces. And everything can and will be used against you (and seldom in your favour).

me.[3] *Chatham House rules apply.*[4] *At the risk of sounding crass, do you think this may have something to do with your ethnicity? As a woman in business,*[5] *I understand and identify with this feeling. Might this be happening, in your view, because you're, for lack of better terms, from Afri … I mean negr … erm, African Ameri … I'm sorry, I mean black?'*[6]

Tracey drops her pen in shock and lifts her head up from her notes. She's looking Tyrone dead in the face. As is Sharon.

Pregnant pause. The room falls as silent as George Washington's enslaved human property on the fourth of July.

You can almost feel Tyrone's heart racing. You can almost hear the sweat trickling down his face. You can see the thoughts of his mortgage, his car loan payments, his annual trip to Miami, his Louboutin trainers, his octoroon girlfriend (and the platinum blonde on the side) all running through his head. He knows what is at stake over the next few seconds: his career, his standard of living, his standing in society and his ability to stand as a man …

Context: Sharon has essentially handed Tyrone a cocked-and-loaded, fully automatic Desert Eagle and invited him to aim it at his own head. He'll either pull the trigger (i.e. say what he really thinks) or put the gun down and live to fight another day (and deny the obvious fact that he considers himself a victim of racism). What will he do?

---

3 No, you cannot.

4 See the previous footnotes. The only rules that apply in a white house are white rules. Fuck Chatham House.

5 White woman in business – there is a difference.

6 Negro, how many times do you have to be told? Don't trust them.

The Story of Tyrone *(continued)*

Following a protracted thinking period, Tyrone coughs twice, sits up and blurts out:

'I'm afraid I do, actually. Especially as I am the only black member of our two and a half thousand-strong staff, I do think this has something to do with my ethnicity, Sharon.'

The End. Literally and figuratively.

If a career was a human being with a brain and a beating heart, by this point medical staff (likely to be low paid and African if they're in Britain) would be cleaning up its remains from the floor. Tyrone just committed career suicide.

Bringing It Back to You

Racism, no matter how glaringly obvious or insidious it may be, will never willingly be acknowledged by a corporation. As long as there is some degree of deniability, regardless how dubious, it will be used to negate the allegation. And there is always *some* degree of deniability. Unless you have a perpetrator wearing a Make America Great Again hat or, at the very least, a man with a swastika tattooed on his forehead, screaming 'DIE THUG NIGGER DIE' while he burns a golliwog hanging from a noose … you're likely to get nowhere.

Even when you are hanging from a tree gasping for dear life by standing on your tippy toes, you'll find Human Resources won't mind taking a punt at saying something like 'Come on. He was just joking when he strung you up. Adolf is a cool guy. Let's all calm down and maintain a sense of perspective and humour.'

The only honourable exception here is if the white person

subjecting you to racism is a totally undesirable employee or someone who rubs management up the wrong way. If he is remotely valuable or popular, like then *Top Gear* star Jeremy Clarkson was to the broadcaster of his TV show when he was caught on tape thundering the only thing black people have ever appropriated from white people (the N-word)[7] and mocking a sitting prime minister's disability[8] and insulting Asians[9] and enraging the Argentines[10] ... some form of 'miracle justification' will be used to protect him.[11] And there is a great chance you are likely to find yourself on the rough side of the experience.

If he is not valuable or popular, he is toast. The company will throw him into a pit of wild rabid anti-racists and laugh as he is ripped limb for limb, opinion piece after opinion piece. The black reward for checkmating a useless white person? You are likely to be Mandela-ised (i.e. upheld as a 'diversity icon'), at least on a temporary basis.

But for the most part, the moment you make a complaint about racism is – chip this in stone – the moment they begin to 'manage you out' of the business.

So, back to Tyrone. The only real politically shrewd non-kamikaze answer to the question 'Do you think this has

7 'Jeremy Clarkson's use of N-word taken very seriously, BBC chief says', *The Guardian*, 15 November 2014.

8 'Jeremy Clarkson apologises for calling Gordon Brown "a one-eyed idiot"', *The Guardian*, 6 February 2009.

9 'Jeremy Clarkson's "slope" joke on *Top Gear* was deliberate use of racist term, Ofcom rules', *Daily Telegraph*, 28 July 2014.

10 '*Top Gear* driven from Argentina after Jeremy Clarkson number plate row', *The Guardian*, 3 October 2014.

11 He was finally sacked when he 'put hands' on an Irish producer (as if it was still the 1800s) for not getting him a late night hot steak after a long hard day of telling racist jokes to camera while driving some planet-killing mobile. 'Jeremy Clarkson apologises to *Top Gear* producer Oisin Tymon', *BBC News*, 24 February 2016.

something to do with your race?' is 'Interesting you should ask; I haven't properly considered that angle.'

And if he really wanted to keep it, as the urban youth say, 'eight more than ninety-two', he could have added: 'You're experienced in this field as a woman in business.[12] What are your suspicions? Do you think race may be a motivating factor here?'

This makes it Sharon's turn to play 'racial Russian Roulette'. Sharon is, of course, either going to refuse to answer or simply say no. Unless, that is, she is insane, totally un-savvy or just one of those truly passionate and honestly good people within an organisation.[13] Or if she is black.

Two-stepping with Racism

Racism is a very serious problem. (Breaking news!) It is real, it damages careers and it destroys lives ... although, to be fair to racism, it does also provide book deal opportunities. But it can literally drive people insane. It kills. So, how do you deal with racism at work? How do you deal with racism in an environment where it is likely to be little understood, largely ignored and certainly not cared for? How do you deal with racism in an environment in which your overarching objective is to acquire power, which in turn requires you to be liked and admired – possibly by people who grew up in societies in which racism is as normal as sand in the Sahara?

The first step is to accept that racism exists and you will

12 White woman in business – there is a difference.
13 Passionate and honestly good people do exist within organisations and companies. They're normally the ones paid to ask if you prefer one or two sugars in your coffee.

experience it, you will be affected by it and you will be enraged by it. Some of it will be on purpose; some of it will be accidental or incidental. However, by accepting and anticipating it, you at least remove the element of surprise and shock. In doing so, you should be prepared to launch into the Whytelaw formula for dealing with racism.

The Whytelaw LDP Formula for Two-stepping with Racism

When faced with racism in the white corporate world, carefully follow the three steps below:

- Step 1: Lie.
- Step 2: Deny.
- Step 3: Pacify.

Example:

Sir Nicholas Griffin IV states that it is an insult to him that you are only paid 20% less than his big white self. He turns to you and says, 'I bet you think I'm racist'.

Model Whytelaw LDP response:

Step 1 (Lie): 'Nick, what are you talking about, mate?! Of course I don't think you sound racist.'

Step 2 (Deny): 'I am not entirely sure pay discrimination exists as a legit concept.'

Step 3 (Pacify): 'I like the fact that you consider me overpaid by twenty per cent because three-fifths, after all, equals to sixty per cent. I admire your grasp of maths.'

Finishing strong is critical. So, you must be ready with your comfort-providing and pacifying fairy tales.

You're either tactful or tactless and tacky. You are building your brand and you have to be seen as someone who can be worked with. Someone likeable. 'One of us'. If you blow up (like Nicki Minaj on *American Idol* or John Sweeney when he tried to be slick with the Scientologists),[14] if you become visibly angry at the first sign of racism, you will struggle to shed the dreaded image of an angry black person. Your career within that organisation (or within the unit of that organisation) is all but over. Cut your losses and move on.

The most potent form of racism the modern black professional will experience will not be of the back-in-the-good-old-days variety. It won't be obvious. It is highly unlikely – though not completely out of the question – that anyone is going to call you the whitest word in the dictionary (the N-word) or insist that you be strapped to a pillar and flogged (unless – in the case of the latter – you're working in Saudi Arabia: the price one pays for tax-free income!). The racism most black professionals will experience will come in the form of lesser access to opportunity, limited ability to progress within an organisation, less pay and someone comparing their post-holiday tan to your natural skin.

The problem with this latterday racism is that its very nature means that it is often hard to substantiate and very easy to deny. The burden of proof is therefore on the victim. The law favours the racist.

In the United Kingdom, racial discrimination lawsuits are only successful 16% of the time.[15] In federal US courts the figure stands at 1% lower than in the UK.[16] So, the whole snapping-

---

14 'Scientology: BBC reporter losing it!': https://www.youtube.com/watch?v=hxqR5NPhtLI.

15 'CULTURE OF DISBELIEF? WHY RACE DISCRIMINATION CLAIMS FAIL IN THE EMPLOYMENT TRIBUNAL', Institute of Race Relations, 2013.

16 'Job-discrimination cases tend to fare poorly in federal court', *Wall Street Journal*, 2009.

and-shouting 'I'm going to call my lawyer on you' approach can prove extremely risky, if not completely futile.

In this environment, the best thing you can do for yourself is to keep a well-protected diary in the hope that eventually it will protect you. Note down moments when you're faced with what you consider to be racism. If there is any proof, email it to yourself. Print it out and take the hard copy home. If necessary, (and legal) use the modern tools of detection and recording: where prudent, safe and, I repeat, legal, subtly record conversations on your mobile phone. Note down the people who witnessed the event.

Once you've compiled your dossier and considered whether or not you can continue to withstand the barrage, if you can't take it any more and absolutely must complain about racism, find a grey-haired lawyer, a civil rights/diversity legend and a social media outrage expert. And accept that it is game over for you in the organisation.

Complaining about racism within the organisation is tantamount to wearing a cherry-red hoodie through a Crip neighbourhood in 1987. The organisation will do what it has to do to protect itself and its most prized asset: its reputation.[17]

Plus, racism, when begrudgingly acknowledged, is damaging and costly to 'unravel'.[18] So, like the gullible westerner and the smoking hot young thing they met on the beach while on holiday, racism and the corporate world are in a sour but seemingly successful marriage. Even if they do want to divorce, the corporate world knows that it's cheaper to

17 This is when black charities become useful. For a small donation many an unscrupulous organisation purchases a good name and forgiveness from these unwitting, unquestioning and often resource poor organisations.

18 'Starbucks anti-bias training: Why the coffee chain closed 8,000 stores', *USA Today*, 29 May 2018. That is, mutate it from one unacceptable form to another more acceptable one.

keep her and, in the interest of balance, financially more comforting to comfort him.

To avoid career-derailing racism, you need to see no racism, hear no racism and speak no racism.

187 Quick Dos and Don'ts: 52–68

52. Do smile politely and nod encouragingly when a colleague says that they 'thoroughly enjoyed' watching *Precious, The Help, The Butler, Roots, 12 Years a Slave* or any other black horror porn.

53. Do cherish that very warm feeling inside when a white colleague says *Django Unchained, Birth of a Nation* or *Get Out* was 'rubbish'.

54. Do pretend as if you are not in favour of reparations. Perhaps you can even throw in a little 'let the past be in the past' or 'people need to stop looking for a handout' or 'it would be impossible to work out who owes what to whom – way more complicated than landing man on the moon'.

55. Do carefully select your news sources. Don't attain your news from Mediatakeout.com, Bossip.com or Dailymail.co.uk (without attaining balance from other sources). If you do, you run the serious risk of becoming a strange compendium of black tomfoolery, trash celebrity culture and absolute white supremacy.

56. Do attain your information and news from thorough and reputable news sources such as the BBC, *New York Times,* CNN, *Wall Street Journal, The Guardian,* gal-dam, *Black Ballad, Media Diversified, Okay Player, Okay Africa, Sahara Reporters,* the *Breakfast Club, British Black List*.

57. Don't confess that you get your news from them. If asked how you stay up to date with current affairs: 'There is no greater and more credible authority on everything than Sean Hannity on *Fox News*. Breitbart is doing God's work. The mere thought of the *Daily Mail* sexually arouses me ... I guess I just love fascism. I can't help it.'

58. Don't ever complain about racism and do pretend racism doesn't exist.

59. Do learn to love racism: because you'll be spending a lot of time with it.

60. Do unto others as they would do unto you, have done unto you and will probably do unto you again.

61. Don't sell yourself short. Always know your worth. And demand it because no one is going to tell you your worth. And no one is going to give it to you voluntarily

62 Do remember that no one will pay you what you're worth. White people pay you what you negotiate, you tolerate and they can get away with. If white people could pay you nothing, they would. And did for hundreds of years.

63. Don't believe that you're the 'highest paid anything' or that 'the company cannot afford it' when they're trying not to give you a pay rise. Demand yours. Get yours.

64. Do set your social media pages to private. Being the queen of memes on black Twitter may feel good socially but professionally it will not endear you to the company at all. The only queen they care about is printed on Sterling.

65. Do act and operate like you're under constant surveillance in the office. You probably are.

66. Don't even think about dating the office intern. Even if he or she is perfectly legal. You are not Bill Clinton; you won't slick-talk your way out of being punished for it.

67. Do draw false moral equivalents when you're made to settle a quarrel between two colleagues. 'You're both right and wrong in equal measure.' If a white man or (especially) a White Man is in the mix, take the side of the White Man. Always. In the event that the argument is White Man vs White Man, don't get involved. Just pray that they both lose. And kill each other.

68. Do carefully study Will Smith in the closing scenes of *Pursuit of Happyness*. Emulate his performance when you're informed that you've passed the probation period for a job. Tear up, break down and show all emotion in an exaggerated manner (the professional equivalent of jumping in the grave at a funeral). Tap dance on the table in celebration if it helps. It provides comfort to the saviour complex in white people.

CHAPTER 7

You Are Not an Activist

'Writer couldn't find a sufficiently racially charged quote.'

– Writer

History matters. And given the history of suppression, slavery, colonialism, Jim Crow, mass incarceration, poor education, naked/covert and institutional racism, Vanilla Ice, etc., activism comes naturally to a remotely 'woke' black person. And how could it not?

Supressing this activism, this rejection of oppression, this reaffirmation of dignity, is therefore often a struggle. In a corporate or professional environment (i.e. when white people in expensive attire are around in an official capacity) this can be problematic.

As a black person it takes effort not to call bullshit when you see it. Especially racist bullshit.

On the chin: everyone knows that you 'have a dream'. But, unless your dream is about how the firm can take little white profits and turn them into big black ones, keep your dream to yourself, Martin. No one cares.

Don't watch *Selma*, *X*, *Birth of a Nation*, *12 Inches a Slave* or any other black liberation flick over breakfast and then make your way into the office pumped at the idea that you're about to lay it down for freedom and justice. Homie, you are not an activist. You are not an opposition politician. You are not on Speakers' Corner on a sunny Sunday afternoon. You are not in the NWA, the new Black Panthers, the Black Mafia Family,[1] the Village People or any other cranky anti-establishment outfit. In fact, you are not remotely anti-establishment (fair enough, you're not the establishment, either). You are not here to change the world or challenge the prevailing order. You are the prevailing order. You are a model professional. You are here to make money and accrue power. Nothing more, nothing less.

White liberal ayatollah Jon Stewart (younger readers, think Trevor Noah, just slightly less ... South African) will happily join the virulently homophobic Westboro Baptist Church before activism and professionalism merge into a progressive single unit. Activism and professionalism are like oil and water, anti-corruption and the oil business, incels and feminists: they just don't mix. Here is why.

The fast track to militant vegan extremism is an eight-hour shift in a sausage factory. If you knew how sausages were made, you'd never put one in your mouth. In fact, you'd probably give up on pork all together. What is true of the sausage-grinding house is true of the corporation. Mashallah.

In order to get that dough, organisations have to create the impression that they are pillars of properness. Large organisations hire teams of lawyers, PR people, compliance officers and, more subtly, private investigators and even outright spies[2] to ensure that they are able to keep a clean image and foresee and curtail any potentially damaging issues. But for some reason, even after hiring all of these well-paid

1 'Young Jeezy, Big Meech, the Black Family Mafia, and a hundred thousand kilos of coke', *Miami New Times*, 6 May 2010.
2 'Harvey Weinstein's Army of Spies', *New Yorker*, 6 November 2017. And 'Inside the secret world of the corporate spies who infiltrate protests', *The Guardian*, 12 December 2017.

(usually white) people and working hard to mitigate the risk of getting caught, corporate scandal after corporate scandal keep breaking in the news. And the reason why isn't that hard to decipher.

In order to attain or retain profitability and perpetual growth,[3] organisations often have to cut corners, to push the law or proper conduct to its very limits. And sometimes they even violate laws, codes of conducts and principles.

This book does not condone or encourage corporate criminality. However, readers should be aware that it exists everywhere. This is reality. Hate it or love it. One day you will more than likely uncover it or notice it. And when you do, because you've been led to believe in the wholesome purity of the company, you, too, won't believe your eyes. Kind of like accidentally walking in on Father Christmas vigorously masturbating.

Where there are steep and unrealistic targets that are linked to a juicy bonus (or at least a pay cheque worthy of the title), there is criminality.

As a result of the near inevitable nature of criminality that is embedded in corporate environments, regardless of how much they may claim otherwise, the last thing any organisation wants or needs is some Che Guevara-Amy Goodman-Paul Mason figure boldly wearing their righteous left-wing credentials on their sleeve, making it all but clear that you can't 'do business' around said person.

'No snitching' isn't the code of the street only. It's the code of the white corporate elite. And they adhere to it a lot better than the streets do, even if they don't wear those down-to-your-knees

---

3 An absolutely ludicrous concept that, by definition, sets everyone up to fail in the long term. But thankfully in the long term we are all dead. The objective is to ensure we don't outlive our good performance run. So, perversely, dying young may be a good career move: it worked for XXXTentacion.

oversized white T-shirts with the words 'Snitches Get Stitches' emblazoned all over them.

White corporate snitches don't get stitches: they just don't get any more jobs.

In the same way you had to make the cool white kids in university comfortable enough to light up weed or crack racist 'jokes' around you, you have to make people feel comfortable enough around you, albeit falsely so, to feel they can commit crimes. People have to be able to let their guard down and bring you into their inner circle. You don't want to be an alienated and depressed Colin Powell sucking his thumb in the corner while bloodthirsty White Men talk about conquering the world.

Nevertheless, you must always demonstrate integrity. Integrity is a massive part of any professional's brand. Few people actually have it, but some can fake the appearance of having it quite successfully.

Part two of the integrity act is creating the impression that you possess the knowledge and grit to 'get things done'. You see and understand the bigger picture. You know how to bury a body if needs be (hopefully not literally, but don't rule it out), how to move money offshore or rig an engine[4] or key interest rate[5] or hack into a dead schoolgirl's mobile[6] or defraud shareholders.[7]

4 'Volkswagen engine-rigging scheme said to have begun in 2008', *New York Times*, 4 October 2015.
5 'Libor rigging trial: Former Barclays bankers jailed', *BBC News*, 7 July 2017.
6 'Missing Milly Dowler's voicemail was hacked by *News of the World*', *The Guardian*, 4 July 2016.
7 'Former Tesco directors charged with fraud over accounting scandal', *The Guardian*, 9 September 2016.

To be absolutely clear and deadly serious, at the risk of insulting the esteemed reader's intelligence: do not commit crimes. Do not agree to commit crimes. Do not become party to criminal activity. Don't get carried away. Especially not in handcuffs.

In a sea of overlooked criminality, the black person has this unbelievable tendency to find themselves in a cold cell for a few decades while everyone else hops away scot-free and rich as a slave master. Even when black involvement was relatively minimal.

The Whytelaw Theory on White-collar Crimes (While Black)

When white professionals are thrown before the justice system for white-collar crimes, juries of all hues tend to look at their careers, their family lives, their performed integrity, their attire, their standard of education and, above all, their skin colour and think, 'I just can't see how this lovely pure white angel would really be stupid enough to place a personal trade right before she placed one for her company account and then sell her personal holding immediately after the company trade increased the share price and made her an immediate profit of £742k. Then she placed the money in her child's account? And then – from there – moved it to her niece and nephew's accounts in the Bahamas – all of which she controls?! Come on. No one white would be that daft and obvious. She went to Durham and is wearing a Versace power suit for God's sake ... she must be innocent!'

In the highly unlikely event they're found guilty,[8] judges and the media tend to be sympathetic.[9]

When a black person is thrown before the justice system for white-collar crimes, you're pretty much just another jail-bound nigger. Not a shame, but a problem (albeit a profitable one). Society (i.e. white people) is already suspicious of successful black people,[10] so it doesn't matter what you wear, how well you're educated, your family structure or the fact that you're a card-carrying Tebbit Tory – it's not looking good. You're black. The judge, the jury, the media and everything in between sees your black skin and purple gums more than they do all of your lovely trimmings. Sympathy is highly unlikely. You might want to pray to white Jesus that he resurrects black Johnnie Cochran to represent you.[11]

Never forget the wise words of Trump (and mafia) lawyer Jay Goldberg: 'prison has a racial overtone'.[12] Which is a highly sanitised way of saying 'jail is for niggers' (JIFN).

8 'White collar prosecutions plummet even as crime rises', *Financial Times*, 23 July 2017.
9 'Libor fraudster Tom Hayes describes prison life in series of letters', *The Guardian*, 3 January 2016.
10 'Serena Williams wants to know why she's drug-tested more than other athletes', *HuffPost*, 2 July 2018.
11 Johnnie Cochran, peace be upon him, was one of the world's greatest lawyers, a proud black man and one hell of a good rhymer.
12 'Let's go back to how a lawyer advising Trump said on CNN that Michael Cohen would be subject to rape with a "racial overtone" in prison', *Slate*, 20 April 2018.

The Story of John, Kweku, Anthony and Constance

Politics, finance and media. Three almost exclusively white professions. And home to the three Great British scandals of the early 21st century. Politicians were found to be fiddling their expenses claims, there was rampant criminality in the financial sector which contributed massively to the 2008 crisis, and sections of the British media were found to be illegally hacking the mobile telephones of people for public titillation (including a kidnapped schoolgirl). Very serious crimes were uncovered but barely anyone went to prison ... except for ...

Surprise of the century: even though each of these sectors have noted 'diversity' problems (which is a cowardly way of saying they have an unofficial the-less-blacks-the-better policy), somehow, in some bizarre way, black people managed to find themselves in the slammer or at least walking away with a criminal record from each of these scandals: Kweku Adoboli in finance,[13] black Conservative Lord Taylor of Warwick (not clear exactly what he was attempting to conserve) in politics[14] and Anthony French in media.[15] Even black judges are not safe: the first judge to be sentenced to prison for more than a hundred years in Britain was Constance Briscoe,[16] one of only two black female judges in the country at the time.

13 'Kweku Adoboli: From "Rising Star" to Rogue Trader', *BBC News*, 20 November 2012.
14 'Ex-Tory peer Lord Taylor jailed for expenses fraud', *BBC News*, 31 May 2011.
15 'Sun reporter Anthony France sentenced over misconduct', *BBC News*, 29 May 2015.
16 'Constance Briscoe jailed for 16 months for lying to police', *BBC News*, 2 May 2014.

In the case of Briscoe, her partners in crime – a major politician and his powerful economist wife – received exactly half of the sentence she was handed even though her involvement in the crime (some overblown infidelity-driven petty dispute over a speeding penalty) was minimal.

In each of these cases, all of the people listed faced absolute ruin with no prospects of reviving their careers (except, that is, the white politician and his white economist wife, who both landed on their feet).

Using Corporate Crime to Your Advantage

JIFN. Jail is for niggers. White people can stab people,[17] hang babies,[18] murder (black) children (ad nauseam), kidnap people and choke them to the point of unconsciousness and then masturbate over them,[19] and commit mass murder[20] and get no jail time. Black people are thrown into prison for offences like taking a bottle of mineral water from a burning building[21] or 'stealing' a lick of ice cream.[22]

17 'Oxford student given suspended sentence for stabbing boyfriend', *The Guardian*, 25 September 2017.
18 'Ex-day care owner gets probation for trying to hang toddler', *CBS News*, 17 July 2018.
19 'Married Alaska air traffic controller, 34, who kidnapped a hitchhiker, choked her until she was unconscious and then masturbated on her is given "a pass" by judge and will not even have to register as a sex offender', *Daily Mail*, 24 September 2018.
20 'Iraq study estimates war-related deaths at 461,000', *BBC News*, 16 October 2013.
21 'College student with no criminal record was jailed for six months on Thursday for stealing a £3.50 case of bottled water during a night of rioting', *Daily Telegraph*, 11 August 2011.
22 'UK riots: Looter jailed for single lick of stolen ice cream', *Metro*, 26 August 2011.

Don't risk it. Just say no to crime, black kids, but don't be oblivious to the fact that you may witness criminality around you. If you do, do not fail to use it to your advantage.

If you witness a crime, especially by someone higher up the corporate food chain than you, use it to clear out the competition. Get rid of a few layers of 'management' and decades of experience above you. Use their criminality to your benefit by reporting it. Write some nice letters to them when they're doing porridge or fighting fungus in jail.

If you want to get ahead, you need to treat your career as a campaign. You still need to be loved. Don't mistake winning a battle, albeit a substantial one that has landed your rivals in jail, for winning the war. And don't mistake winning the war for winning the peace. Make sure you strategise to the bitter end, even when the competition are joining prison gangs for protection.

As opposed to claiming the bounty yourself, as a result of reporting the crime yourself, it may be prudent to tip off the office freedom fighter (or manoeuvre the information into his or her hands) and let them inform 'the poh-lease' or call the whistleblowing hotline.

The office freedom fighter will feel good about their successful crusade against corporate crime and brag of their 'public service' when queuing up for the dole (or basking in their glorious Twitter mentions) and you'll feel good about your improved status within the organisation. And the hard, cold cash that goes with it. Everyone is a winner, baby. Except for the poor souls in prison, of course. But they're criminals, remember – society's failures. Sapien trash. Feel no remorse, for they would feel none for you.

Fuck them, for they would royally fuck you in a heartbeat.

Clear out the criminal competition but leave more than enough distance between you and the crime reporter for you to reap the rewards.

Never forget: you are not an activist. You are not in the organisation to hold power or powerful people to account (even if you're a journalist or – forbid the wretched thought – a compliance officer). You are there to attain the power, not to fight it.

187 Quick Dos and Don'ts: 69–85

69. Don't ever say (let alone believe) that 'this job is all I have' (it's not) or 'this job saved my life' (it didn't). It is a fucking job. If you lose it, you will survive and thrive – unless, that is, you were once a rapper and still have a gang name tattooed on your face. If that is the case, then yes, the job is all you have.

70. Do pretend as if white-on-white violence doesn't exist and that white-people-land is a crime-free, drug-free place of peace, harmony, 0.1% unemployment and absolute protection from climate change.

71. Don't ever agree to help a colleague procure drugs. Be firm on this. To him or her it will be a bit of fun; to you it could spell a very long time in prison. And he/she will not visit you or put money on your books. He/she may even go full white and testify against you.

72. Don't bitch-slap a colleague in anger when they act surprised by the fact that you don't take drugs and/or have never sold drugs.

73. Do write down and remember the Whytelaw formula on drugs:
- White skin + drugs = rehabilitation, sympathy, redemption and/or a loving funeral
- Black skin + drugs = a cold jail cell, a pillow between your gnashing teeth, absolute unemployability, punchline

fodder and, finally, being thrown into an unmarked hole or into the sea.

74. Don't cry in shame or freeze in surprise when you see your colleagues, your goddamned white colleagues, congregating round a computer laughing their heads off at a WorldStarHipHop buck fight or hood rat brawl. Black people beating the shit out of each other has been a form of entertainment for white people for millennia.

75. Do ensure that you have a clear understanding of white supremacy before you embark on a professional career. Doing so will help maintain your sanity.

76. Do keep your love for the works of moderate whites like Michael Moore, John Pilger, Owen Jones, Naomi Klein and Tim Wise to yourself.

77. Don't go postal (like a bearded white man) when a white colleague looks you dead in the eye and asks, 'Who is the definitive, unquestionable and undisputed greatest rapper ever: Eminem, Macklemore or any of the guys in the Beastie Boys?'

78. Don't be swayed by tough, emotive talk or even crazed thug talk during salary negotiations. The job of the salary/contract negotiator is to acquire your labour for as cheap a price as possible.

79. Don't respond to your boss's sweet memories of his days as a 1% Hell's Angel by revealing that you were a Piru Blood 'back in the day'.

80. Do mask your desperate opportunism and nationalism. The more you're able to pretend that you absolutely love all the symbols, statues, cultural activities, strange practices and values white people hold dear, the better you'll fare economically, socially and mentally.

81. Don't wear your hat backwards, sag, wear a boob tube,

a dashiki or anything too baggy or too tight or too black on dress-down day. It may be better not to dress down on dress-down day at all – keep it corporate (not couture).

82. Don't ever forget that words speak much louder than actions ... when it comes to racism. So, if your boss pays you 10% of what he'd pay a white man: not racist. If he accidentally uses the phrase 'coloured people' to describe 'people of colour' he pushed the racism button and must be immediately castrated.

83. Don't ever threaten to resign. Just do it.

84. Do beware of the 'people of colour'/'BAME'/'all ethnics are the same' scam. These 'coalitions' are often used to disguise anti-black discriminatory practices. '10% of our senior leaders or 300 people are BAME,' said the CEO of No Negros Inc. What he didn't say is that only two of those 300 people are black: the Head of Door men and Head of Diversity).

85. Don't mistake the emergence and inevitable re-emergence of 'diversity' as a corporate buzzword (often accompanied with 'embrace' and 'celebrate') as being a sign of upcoming betterment for black professionals.

CHAPTER 8

Pick Your Battles

'Better to be judged by 12 than carried by six ...'

– Philosophy of the Drive-by

Y ou know that person in the office who always seems to be in drama? Always seems to be either moments away from a heated argument or in the middle of one? The Tupac Shakur of the office – and by this I do not mean the 'Keep Ya Head Up' Tupac, I mean 'Hit 'Em Up' Tupac.

You don't? Then it is probably you.

Whether in a personal or professional setting, we all know that person. The person who is always in some form of skirmish or another. Even when they're not actually involved in drama, it still feels like they are.

These folks may in fact be lovely ice-cream- and dandelion-sharing angels when you get to know them, but most of us, especially in a professional setting, will not spare the time or effort to find that out. Once the clock hits five-ish, said person is, at best, dinner-party fodder.

So that one-off, unfortunate and out-of-character occasion when the Office Tupac loses their shit becomes synonymous with their reputation as a professional. That's what people know them for, that's what they remember and what they expect. That is their brand.

Brands are, after all, shaped by what sticks in the mind. Advertisers are paid shedloads of money to make consumers remember and desire their client's brand. They use all sorts of ridiculousness to achieve this. The jingle, the quirky talking animal, the past-it cokehead celebrity, quack science, the empty slogan ('You're worth it'), racism, extreme objectification of women, the Kardashians, appropriation of anti-police brutality movements.[1] Whatever it takes, the advertiser just needs to ensure that you, the brain-dead consumer, remembers the advert and therefore their client's product within a few expensive seconds of airtime.

The same goes for professionalism. Your career is only as good as those few expensive seconds of airtime you get with management. And if management are using that time not to fine-tune your bright ideas – or the ideas of the person you 'relieved' them from – but to surgically remove your foot from someone else's rear end, then they will know you as a problem employee. Not a profitable or promising one.

Any company worthy of respect, regardless of how minor or major it may be, will always hammer on about how their 'reputation' (though what they really mean is 'brand') is their most valuable asset. It's the same for any professional. Once you've developed your reputation (brand), whether justly or not, it is very hard, if not impossible, to alter it.

And, as I'm sure you've guessed, it's even more difficult to shed a negative brand if you're the odd chocolate chip in a bath tub of vanilla milkshake.

1 'Pepsi pulls controversial Kendall Jenner ad', *CNN*, 5 April 2017.

The Story of Kanye (aka Kanye Bomaye!)

Kanye West. The artist formerly known as Kanye West. Ye. Whatever he calls himself, he is an unmitigated musical genius. Once the toast of the music industry. But beyond just being a well-liked music icon-in-the-making, Kanye achieved something quite rare for a rapper. In fact, he achieved something quite rare for anyone (but especially for a black person): he became an all-American sweetheart.

And nothing crystallised his sweetheart status more than when his mother passed away.

The death of Kanye's mother was afforded the reverence and respect that is usually reserved for undeservedly revered white people (like Ronald Reagan, the Queen's mother and, Britain's greatest TV presenter and charity fundraiser ever, Sir Jimmy Saville[2]). International media caringly covered it. Even in the stiff upper-lipped, hideously white and snobbish British media, time and space was found to speak about Kanye's mother's passing during the influential, national agenda-setting 10 p.m. news bulletins across multiple mainstream (i.e. white) TV channels.

It was his time. Kanye was on autopilot (and Auto-Tune). The lovable negro of the moment. But, sadly, as he soon learned, all-American sweethearts are not equal.

He felt that very black urge to self-destruct by the easiest means possible: telling white people the truth. This, of course, is a huge no-no for all black professionals: never tell white people the truth.

He needlessly and pointlessly chose to attack another American sweetheart – some white singer with blonde hair

---

2 It would be criminally remiss not to mention that Jimmy Saville was also the most prolific and committed paedophile ever to inhale Britain's fresh air.

and long legs – by snatching the microphone out of her hand at an international award show and telling her that some singing black woman was more deserving of an award she had just received. This was easily the biggest strategic error by an ethnic since Saddam invaded Kuwait.

Kanye's war crimes:

- *Being anything less than absolutely deferential to a blonde;[3]*
- *Questioning the supremacy of white people;*
- *Telling white people the truth;*
- *Mistaking the MTV Awards for the Source Awards. To be fair, if he'd pulled this stunt at the Source Awards he would have been shot right then and there;*
- *And probably most importantly, messing with white folk's money.*

Overnight, his image changed. Kanye went from all-American sweetheart to all-African American philistine. From a black guy so lovable he could have been a recurring

---

3 White Men and white men alike will commit murder for blondes. For example, the reason for the 1961 assassination of the great freedom fighter and post-Independence Congolese leader Patrice Lumumba is often chalked up to many things. His absolute refusal to bow before the Belgians, his willingness to deal with Russians, his forthright nature, his 'inability' to transit from activist to statesman are amongst them. I, Whytelaw, however, chalk it up to a chance evening in Washington. After a long day of erratic negotiation, he reportedly asked the State Department's Congo desk officer, Thomas Cassilly, for a female companion for the night. When asked what sort of lady he would like, Lumumba reportedly responded: *'une blanche blonde'*. The CIA – according to Martin Meredith's book *The State of Africa* – duly acted on the procurement request and Lumumba expressed 'complete satisfaction'. Their next alleged Lumumba-related procurement was his assassination.

guest on Friends[4] *to Muhammad Ali on that conveniently forgotten episode of* Parkinson *(where he, too, felt that very black urge to tell white people the truth).*

Yeezus and Ye aside, he was still making good music, but he wasn't the heart-warming Grammy-sweeping Prince Charming he once was. The feeling was gone. These days his musical prowess and legacy are widely ignored and his brand has been reduced to an increasingly angry and crazed clothes horse, who has married a woman famous for making a sex tape with a pint-sized minor singer with a python-sized black penis (according to millions of reliable sources).

Somewhat surprisingly, Kanye appears to have embraced his jackass role in society. He now seems to enjoy acting the fool and locking horns with pretty much everyone and anyone, including our enslaved black ancestors.[5] Possibly on purpose. But he can afford to. He can afford to engage in conflict, even proactively, and show his ass and ignorance. And so can you, but only if you have what he has: power. Also, he is a rapper, so being an unhinged jackass is part of the job description.

The key thing to remember from the story of Kanye: conflict sticks in the mind. It is a very simple way to flush your brand and career down the toilet.

As a result of this, the black professional must take extra care not to inadvertently invite conflict. Avoid needless wise-cracks, don't remind white people that yoga is a form of cultural appropriation, don't say 'coffee kills' and don't ever mention

4 A pre-Obama era, widely revered and painfully dour no-blacks-allowed TV show.
5 'Kanye West just said 400 years of slavery was a choice', *CNN*, 1 May 2018.

Bob Dylan's Christmas album or, even worse, Eminem's risible 2018 albums. Don't tell white people the truth about anything. Especially not about themselves. Just tell them what they want to hear. It is a catalyst to a comfortable and peaceful black life.

Should you end up in a battle in a professional setting, remember, white people are like cheap Thai rice: they stick together.

Managing Conflict

You have to pick your battles wisely. If you don't, they will pick you. Sometimes they will pick you anyway. Conflict is a certainty. In the same way that you will not go through your personal life without conflict, you will not go through your career without it either. It may not be as certain as tax, death and – if you're black – police harassment, but it's fairly close.

To manage conflict is to manage your career trajectory. But managing conflict is a carefully nurtured skill. Like racism, religion and stomaching Paul McCartney collaborations with black artists, managing and avoiding conflict isn't something you're born knowing how to do. Everyone has to learn it and most people don't. To the person who has learned to manage conflict effectively, the ignorance of others represents a clear advantage that must be ruthlessly exploited.

Conflict shouldn't be viewed as something negative. Not in the slightest. And certainly not by the black professional. It is a double-edged sword: it can work against you, but, if you know how to use and manage it, conflict could be the making of you.

Managing conflict should never be mistaken for peacekeeping. In fact, it may actually require you to focus some of your energy on warmongering. You are not the United Nations. You are the motherfucking United States and the United Kingdom, getting your Bush 'n' Blair on. Getting your uber-White Man on.

Effectively managing conflict is simply the art of ensuring that you are, and remain, everyone's 'friend' while anyone who poses a potential threat to your objectives, to your rise to power, is at someone else's throat or permanently bogged down with time- and energy-draining confrontations. The more your rivals look and sound like crazed Tupacs outside the court house spitting at the press and yelling 'have a great summer, beyaaatch', the better.

Real talk: to effectively manage conflict is to divide, manipulate and therefore rule. And make them say 'Thank you, sir' for all of the above. Get your White Man on, youngster.

Now, if that sounds brutal to you, then that's because it is. But it is also undeniably brilliant. The history of conquered, enslaved and colonised people of African descent is the history of effective dividing, ruling and stealing of resources. And, indeed, people.

So, feel no remorse in implementing your own divide-and-rule strategy in your company or organisation. It is a necessary evil. Like building empires, making omelettes or visiting the loo at a white music festival, acquiring power is not a pretty or clean business. If it helps relax the soul, the black professional should view it as correcting historical wrongs. In addition, that is, to cold-blooded, shrewd and relentless capitalism.

The objective for you is to ensure that rivals are at each other's throats. Don't go too far (especially if people are allowed to carry guns in your country or state) but go far enough to keep them too busy to perform well and think straight. Go far enough to make them look a tiny bit crazy and erratic. Enough to drive them a little bit Britney Spears during her impromptu neo-Nazi haircut phase rather than full-blown Miley Cyrus gone rogue twerking wigger.

187 Quick Dos and Don'ts: 86–102

86. Do resist the urge to have the 'model minority' employee assassinated. If you play your cards right, play the game and abide by every squalid manoeuvre suggested in this book, you could be the model minority soon.

87. Do take elocution classes, if required. There is little worse than dressing like Barack and Michelle only to open your mouth and sound like Cardi B and Offset or Ricky and Bianca.

88. Do master how to speak corporate jargon. It is usually point-less and used to disguise the fact that you don't know what you're talking about, but coming from the lips of a negro it is essentially like watching magic being performed.

89. Don't be fooled by a person speaking corporate jargon. They're often hiding the fact that they don't know what they're talking about.

90. Do go somewhere you've never been every year. More importantly, go somewhere once a year where you're not a black person, but a person, i.e. go to a country at least visibly dominated by black people. Consider it a sanity-maintaining detoxification trip.

91. Don't allow yourself to become a company diversity mascot without getting something in return. If you're sat near the entrance, pictured on the company website, featured in the company advert and pointlessly placed before important clients, at least make sure you get paid for your 'diversity services'.

92. Don't fuck someone for professional expediency reasons. There are too many reasons why this is a bad idea.

93. Don't put the interests of a company before your own. Unless you own the company.

94. Don't mistake your loitering for loyalty. Loyalty and loitering sound and often look alike but, like estranged twins, they couldn't be more different. Loyalty is rewarded in kind; loitering isn't rewarded at all.

95. Don't hesitate to play dumb. Creating a false sense of comfort around you makes people feel comfortable enough to be themselves around you. This is weakness: exploit it.

96. Don't forget that you can't buy or skip experience. You either have it or you don't, and it will eventually show.

97. Don't know your place or stay in your place. Be ambitious, be audacious and be industrious.

98. Don't sell yourself short at all. And don't be too short-sighted.

99. Do aim too high. Otherwise you're not aiming high enough.

100. Don't show up for the professional equivalent of nuclear warfare with a spear. Be prepared and properly equipped for all eventualities.

101. Don't overstay your welcome. And don't let others do the same.

102. Do treat Human Resources like a big butt and a smile, a flat ass and a frown, or a clean-shaven brother with a fucked-up hairline (think Kwasi Kwarteng): with extreme suspicion. Do. Not. Trust. Them. For they will be your smiling and charming benevolent cremators.

CHAPTER 9

White Guilt

'Race has nothing to do with it.'

– White people (c.1456 to date)

White guilt is the myth of individual or collective guilt felt by white people for harm resulting from the racist treatment of non-whites by whites both historically and currently.

Sadly, it doesn't exist in any professional setting. It's a myth.

Accept it, prepare for the absolute worst and, if the worst doesn't kill you, move to Atlanta. Seek therapy.

PART 2

OVERTHROWING THE WHITE MAN

'In this country in fifteen or twenty years'
time the black man will have the whip
hand over the white man.'

— Enoch Powell, 'Rivers of Blood' speech (1968)

'Amen.'

— The church

CHAPTER 10

It's Not Just What You Do, It's Who You Do It in Front Of

'Whoever exalts himself will be humbled, and whoever humbles himself will be exalted.'

– Jesus Christ, revolutionary black man

Many people within organisations – sometimes even the best – never really rise to their true potential. Not because they are bad at their jobs – quite the contrary – but because they are selfless and giving. They believe the garbage about working hard (as opposed to working smart) and getting somewhere as a result. They throw their pearls before swine and usually end their careers bitter. And poor. And then they develop addictions to heroin, crack, crystal meth or viral motivational quotes on the internet. And then they die. In debt.

So why do they fail? Why do better armies with superior weaponry lose wars? Why did England (a team without a single world-renowned player) perform much better in the 2018 World Cup than football superpowers Spain, Germany, Argentina, Nigeria and Portugal? Why did the well-oiled

Clinton machine lose to the pussy-grabbin' Trump band-wagon? Why did David beat Goliath? Why did Theresa May's 'strong and stable' Tory party blow a 25-point lead over Jeremy Corbyn's 'divided and derided' Labour party in a snap election she called?

Simple. They failed to effectively strategise.

You must strategise. On the macro and micro levels. You must have a broad long-term strategy, but you also need to be ready for those small minute-to-minute and day-to-day moments which make up the long term. You must have a game plan. And a contingency game plan for when the initial one blows up in your face, jihadi-style. Because it will.

And remember, especially if you're black, you've got to be loved. So critical to strategising for the black professional is creating the impression that you're not strategising. Everyone has to think that your good fortune is just a matter of luck,[1] sheer hard work and being in the right place at the right time. Or being down to bullshit 'diversity initiatives' or affirmative action.

So, how does strategising work in practice?

'If a tree falls in a forest and no one is around to hear it, does it make a sound?'[2]

This question is, according to the pillar of factual reliability that is Wikipedia, a philosophical thought experiment that

---

1 'Luck is being prepared when opportunity presents itself' – Hasim Rahman, a journeyman boxer who knocked out boxing great Lennox Lewis with what Lewis described as a 'lucky punch'. 'Luck' or 'preparedness' or 'opportunity' were not on Rahman's side during the rematch. Lewis flattened him.

2 An alternative question could be 'If the police shoot a brother in the back while handcuffed and then take the cuffs off him and say he did it to himself, should it still be considered suicide?'.

raises questions about observation and our knowledge of reality.

This experiment is worth employing in corporate environments. It is reminiscent of what happens every day. A person does a great piece of work and gets no credit, no bump, for it. Why? Because no one witnessed it.

And by 'no one' I mean no one who matters.

Doing a great piece of work or coming up with a great idea is useless unless it is done within eye- or earshot of someone who can, and probably will, do something to propel you forward in return. So, a smart professional only does things that really matter in front of people who matter. Reserve your best thoughts and ideas for those rare moments when you're in earshot of the shot-caller.

Your career progression is essentially a series of rare and extremely short periods of facetime with senior and influential members of staff. (Note: key staff members can be senior as well as junior staff members. But they are usually white.) You cannot afford to waste any moment you get with the big cheeses. Each time you're with a key member of staff, you have to impress them with either your professional or social expertise. You have to leave a lasting good impression.

So, for those moments that you'll be alone with, or in close proximity to, one of the stars of the game, have something, or preferably some things, ready to talk about. Try to find out what they're interested in or what you have in common. And keep bringing it up. Memorise the names of their ugly pets or their rotten kids or their parents' ailments and ask about them ('Morning, Doug. Your grandmother sorted out her syphilis yet?'). Engage in painful sports-related banter, even if you hate sport. Take up an implicitly whites-only sport like golf (and enjoy hitting that white ball as hard as you can). Whatever it takes, just make sure you build familiarity and camaraderie.

In order to do this, you will need to demonstrate a degree of empathy and sincerity.[3]

You Have to Pick a Pocket or Two

Professionally speaking, you are only as good as your ideas. Or someone else's. Your carefully thought-through and well-protected ideas are as precious as gold. In fact, they are gold. And so are everyone else's. However, if someone is in the mood to be charitable by leaving their safe open, then see to it that you're the main beneficiary of their charity. Take their idea, polish it up and make it yours. Then act like it was yours all along. That's the American way.

After all, you are going to be 'relieved' of your ideas (just as your forebears were theirs) with either a smile from a (probably white) peer or the strong arm of seniority. So, you shouldn't give a second's thought to doing it to someone else. Especially not someone with the oppressor gene in them.

This is a hallmark of all large and successful corporations. There is hardly a product that Apple, for example, has rolled out, from the iPod to the iPhone and the iPad, that wasn't already in existence in some form or fashion. They just perfected it, heavily branded it, created an unrivalled customer experience and watched the money pile up. No idea is original, after all. Some inventions are, however, patented.

A former colleague, who happened to be a well-regarded senior manager at one of the largest asset managers in the world, had a great strategy for idea appropriation. He was lazy

3 'Once you fake the sincerity the rest is easy' – unknown, but often credited to Tony Blair.

and mediocre for the most part but he understood the game. He was a master at the pre-meet game.

His game plan was simple, standardised and slick: before any meeting with company White Men he would ensure that he had a discussion with junior members of staff. The very purpose of this pre-meet was to steal ideas.

The first meeting was arranged to helpfully 'try to ensure that you had your responses ready for senior management', which was only half true. In reality he was trying to ensure their ideas were good enough for him. The moment they were in the actual meeting with the most important people in the company and being asked for their thoughts, he'd kindly pipe up on his juniors' behalf.

'Allow me to help with that one,' he would say.

Then he'd launch into a great response: your response, your ideas. At the end of the meeting, after everyone had left, even though you'd said nothing, he'd praise you to high heaven for coming up with such a great idea. Right when it didn't matter.

He did what is done in business: he strategised. He strategically took your ideas and made them his. He took your gown and wore it to the ball. Took unchewed meat from your mouth and swallowed it. Ruthless. Yet he still managed to make you feel good about yourself afterwards.

That is the very best form of strategising: robbing someone and then making them feel as if you gave them a gift. The risk of comeuppance is curtailed.

The moral of the story: do not waste time on the hard work. You must remain a good performer/actor. But don't be deluded: hard work doesn't garner success. Take the case of first-generation African migrant Mr Kunta Kinte as an example. His white workmates struggled to pronounce his name so they took the liberty of warmly referring to him as Toby. Kunta kindly agreed to call himself Toby too. He was an exceptionally hard worker and he never let his disability or fluid family situation get in the way of his performance. It didn't help one bit. He was treated like he worked for Sports Direct.[4] And worked literally until he dropped.

With the exception of perhaps some sports, in almost any industry the person who sweats the most gets paid the least. Hard work doesn't garner success. Smart work does. Focus purely on the work that will get you rewarded, that will get you noticed by people who can do something for you. Kindly delegate anything that has little-to-no career progression value.

C'mon, after 500 years of free hard work, it is time to let others have a turn.

4 'Sports Direct working conditions like a "Victorian workhouse", says damning report', *Daily Mirror*, 22 July 2016.

187 Quick Dos and Don'ts: 103–120

103. Do enjoy the journey. For all of the pain, failure, racism, being mistaken for 'the help', 'the butler' or the prostitute, it is the journey that matters ... on a therapist's sofa.

104. Do note that any anti-racism or diversity body that draws its funding from the exact same organisations it is supposed to be holding to account or diversifying is not an anti-racism or diversity body. It's a public relations scam.

105. Don't be offended when white people are treated as greater authorities on the general black experience than you are. Like most things, it began in Africa. Most people in Africa are black; most 'experts' on Africa are white.

106. Do call it a day if you find yourself singing and/or humming a modern old-negro spiritual at your desk. Examples include: 'Golden' by Jill Scott, Labi Siffre's version of 'Something Inside So Strong', any number of songs by Common, etc.

107. Do keep a diary, a good lawyer's details and a Haitian voodoo doll within reach.

108. Do arm yourself with K-Y Jelly if the head of your company keeps evoking the word 'family' when referring to the company. When you hear the word 'family' it means the White Man is preparing to buy himself a new Ferrari.

109. Do beware of the latest rebranding and marketing scheme for racism. For example: 'unconscious bias' is often very conscious racism, where there is a 'lack of diversity' there is an abundance of racism, 'did you notice that "identity politics" suddenly became all the rage in the latter days of the Obama years.'

110. Do note that there is a clear inverse relationship between the level of total compensation and how intoxicated a company keeps their staff.

111. Do be prepared to be thoroughly insulted and disrespected whenever the words 'no disrespect, but ...' are thrown in your direction – especially during salary negotiations.

112. Do remember that no matter how many times white people get things wrong and no matter how wrong they may be, they can still draw from a bottomless ocean of credibility. As far as black people are concerned, once you spill your shot glass of credibility you're going to die of thirst.

113. Do remember that 80% of success is showing up ... in white skin. And 80% of getting the door slammed in your face is showing up in black skin. Either way, it is very much worth showing up. There are only so many times a door can be smashed in your face before you say, 'Fuck a door. I'm building my own mansion.'

114. Do offer loyalty when you see that it could earn you some royalties (and only then). But always create the impression that you're as slavishly loyal as a modern British prime minister is to their American presidential counterpart.

115. Don't mistake a bad day in the office for a bad life. Don't mistake a bad boss or colleagues for a bad company.

116. Don't feel disheartened if you're informed that a company treats their employees 'like animals'. White people have long treated animals better than black people.

117. Don't needlessly go into debt. Every penny you spend that you don't own is the tightening of the noose round your neck.

118. Do nod in faux agreement (while biting your lip) when you're told that free market capitalism toppled apartheid and slavery (as opposed to the Haitians chopping the White Man's head clean off).

119. Do buy property before you buy a nice car. Especially if you live in London, New York, San Francisco or anywhere else where the property market is an orgy of money laundering and profitability.

120. Do note that the point above is not financial, investment or legal advice. The value of your property may go up as well as down ... especially when white people and Hollywood-villain white people start squabbling again.

CHAPTER 11

Network (i.e. Gossip and Make Fake Friends)

'White supremacy will be strengthened, not weakened, by women's suffrage.'

– Carrie Chapman Catt, a crusader for women's suffrage and founder of the League of Women Voters

'I thought the bitch was WHITE! God damn it! I thought the bitch was white. Fuck!'

– Roseanne Barr after being fired by a black woman for racially abusing another black woman

Show me a person who repeatedly visits the water cooler for thirstation purposes only and I'll show you a pending bankruptcy.

The location of the water cooler or the coffee machine or microwave is perhaps the most important place in any office. Empires are built, destroyed and occasionally rebuilt there. This is the focal point of action. The water cooler was the highway of information that existed before the internet and will exist long after the internet has been overthrown by some other medium of stealing intellectual property and watching porn for free. Why? Because the water cooler is where gossip is exchanged.

Gossip Is the Currency of Professionalism

You've either got it or you're bankrupt. You're either exchanging gossip with others or, forbid the thought, you are the subject of the gossip. It's what keeps the office exciting. And depressing.

As a result of centuries of horrendous publicity, the gossip (both the deliverer and the actual tittle-tattle) has severely negative social connotations. Even your mother is likely to have warned you that 'no one likes a gossip'. Well, Mum was wrong again. Everyone likes a gossip because everyone, at some point or another, is gossiping.

'Don't tell anyone but …' Like hell you won't.

You buy trashy tabloid newspapers and read titillation websites because you love gossip. You've probably googled your ex-lover (and their new partner) this very morning because you love a little gossip. (Of course, you may also still be in love with him/her. Or you just miss the sex.)

Because gossip validates or invalidates us. We need it. We need to know. We are human and therefore prone to error and insecurity. And addiction and yo-yo diets. We need to know if we are up or down against another person. We need to know if our miserable existence has just been weakened or enhanced by even greater adjustments in another person's existence.

Peeling it back to the basics, gossip is little more than the morally dubious dissemination of information before it becomes 'actual information'. It's basically 'the inside story', 'the word on the street', 'the hook-up'. On some days, it's just lies. Either way, in the realm of professionalism it serves a valid purpose.

If information is power and, as Chairman Mao, a man responsible for the deaths of millions, opined, power is wielded from the barrel of a gun, then gossip is a nuclear warhead waiting to be delivered.

Gossip – how it is delivered and who it is delivered to/by – is a huge part of what constitutes power. You must acquire it and exchange it sensibly and sparingly.

This is what makes the water cooler the offshore seat of power in an organisation. The Enola Gay of the office. As long as they have existed, the water cooler and other similar points of dubious congregation have served as the key location for gossiping. (Note: in this instance, 'dubious congregation' is not a subtle reference to brothels … or the Catholic Church.) That is not going to change any time soon. These days, offices worth their salt wouldn't be caught dead with an actual water cooler but the iPad-powered coffee dispenser, sparkling water gun, etc. serve the same purpose.

But gossip goes beyond – far beyond – the simple dissemination of who is sleeping with whom or who is up for promotion or decapitation: it is a sign that you are effectively networking.

If you don't know the gossip, you're not effectively networking. And every professional is only as strong as their network.

What Is a Professional Network?

Some would define a network (or 'networking') as a loosely organised group of people within an organisation or industry who have come together, perhaps informally, to help better themselves professionally and improve their standing, career-wise.

Cutting through the bullshit, networking is merely creating a group of 'friends', most, if not all of them, fake, with the desire to ensure that they:

- Feel some form of loyalty towards you;
- Tip you off on the big issues coming your way;

- Defend you when it inevitably goes down;

- Introduce you to other people who could be useful to you;

- Assist with your ascension to the top;

- Defend you from obvious racism, as you can't effectively and robustly do it for yourself (see Chapter 5);

- And, most importantly, share the gossip with you.

Show me your network and I'll show you your net worth.

Nevertheless, don't get fooled or fool yourself into thinking people in your network are your deep personal friends. They're not. This is a group of people who have come together to provide mutually beneficial career 'services' for one another. Treat it like a series of one-night stands. Make sure it works for you more than it does for them. Breaking even is acceptable. A few loss leaders may be necessary.

The more senior, influential and white your network is, the better. Your promotion, your progress, your pertinence and your pay will be determined by these people. Might as well have them in your pocket, right?

Well, yes and no. It all comes down to how they became senior.

'Befriending' merit-based senior management folk poses significant risks. They are usually swift to smell bullshit, as they are likely to be classic bullshit merchants themselves. And they may also have a dying need to demonstrate their integrity (and by inadvertent extension their insecurity) by being that little bit harder on their 'personal friends'.

You may be better off ingratiating the friend of the competent senior manager into your network. Let him take the heat, put in a good word for you and attend the unbearable nights out. Or, God forbid, the unsolicited come-ons. You just stay on the good side of the senior manager, make sure he (and it will, almost inevitably, be a he) knows you to be a capable pair of hands and never give him any chance to doubt it.

As for the senior manager who just landed there as a result of one privilege or another, the quicker you have that sucker in your back pocket the better. There is no downside to associating with this guy. If a 'trophy employee' like the third cousin of the future King of England works for your company, make him your best friend immediately. It will only serve to propel your career.

Finally, no general wants to find out that his troops are flabby and sick just as a hostile army is invading. So, you should always take measures to test your network. Make sure your crew are not weak. Find out how loyal or battle-prepared they are. In doing so, you'll be able to ascertain how much they value your 'friendship'.

A good example of corporate 'war games' would be to plant some gossip about yourself purposefully in a manner that ensures it will fall into the ears of your network. Nothing too crazy: 'Boulé is a cynophilic R. Kelly fan' would be going a little too far. Something stinging and plausible but not terminally damaging. You can figure it out yourself. Once the seed's been planted, see if it works its way back to you in the form of a heads-up. If not, unless you know that a particularly stalwart colleague has quashed the rumour before it could spread, your network is not that loyal to you, not battle-ready and not fit for purpose. You will need to rectify this very quickly or you will be exposed and vulnerable.

Like all war games, this is very risky territory, so think it through very carefully. This is not for the faint-hearted or the sloppy.

187 Quick Dos and Don'ts: 121–137

121. Don't ever acknowledge that racism or white supremacy may be at the root of your woes. Even if it is blindingly obvious that it is. To *not* blame racism is to be seen as 'strong' and 'admirable' in the 'face of overwhelming adversity'. To blame it is to be seen to be intellectually weak and full of excuses. If need be, smile and yell, 'DON'T WORRY! RACE HAS NOTHING TO DO WITH IT!' as you're hung from the company tree by your 'conservative' boss.

122. Do smile to yourself when you hear for the thousandth time that 'something doesn't feel right' about Meghan Markle.

123. Don't mistake the black boss for a saviour. He may well put shinier and tighter shackles on you.

124. Do expect to be mistaken for other black people. And don't ever give the impression that you're offended by it. One nigger is all niggers.

125. Do expect to be judged by other black people's mistakes. One nigger is all niggers.

126. Do laugh at the boss's jokes. Even if they're depressingly white, i.e. unfunny. It boosts his ego and makes him think that you like him – critical to career progression.

127. Do remember that black folk don't ever have 'emotional breakdowns' or make 'cries for help'. So, if you're a little too strident with your office furniture like your white male colleague was during his 'moment of distress', it will be considered a 'cry for a brown box' ... and a grey prison cell.

128. Do expect to be defined by the minority perspective beneficial to white people. A thousand black people may have an overwhelmingly negative perspective of the firm;

however, that one brother or sister who has a 'positive' point of view (i.e. the point of view white people want to hear) will be the one used to define the experience of the thousand.

129. Do make a lot of noise when you've made even the most minor of achievements. If you don't promote yourself no one else will.

130. Do keep any view that is counter to popular narrative (i.e. white narrative) to yourself. Kate Moss and Brad Pitt can't wash Bria Myles and Morris Chestnut's socks in the looks department? MLK was murdered only after he started focusing on reparations and economic justice? Keep that stuff firmly to yourself.

131. Do pick your poison in relation to pay secrecy. Don't ask colleagues what they're paid (unless you can handle the bitter truth). Not because it's impolite but because it is likely to throw you off the rails when you find out that they're paid significantly more than you (if they're white). Nevertheless, do note that pay secrecy is the very best friend of pay discrimination.

132. Don't be anything less than supremely professional on email. Don't vent on email. Don't put someone in their place on email. Don't share a secret on email. Don't even respond to a hostile email – on email. There is no remedy for email: bad emails always come back to savage you.

133. Do be discreet with your personal information. Anything black you say can and almost certainly will be used to destroy you.

134. Don't mistake an ally for a friend. Just because your interests are aligned today doesn't mean they always will be.

135. Don't mistake constructive criticism for hatred. Or hatred for criticism. It's critical you recognise which is which.

136. Do note that only white men are ever hired unquestionably on merit. And they never run out of merit. Even if they never had any to begin with.

137. Do not underestimate the power and appeal of pull-your-pants-up politics. Pulling your pants up is, apparently, the silver bullet that resolves all problems associated with being black.

CHAPTER 12

Sex Sells

'Purse first, ass last.'

Sex appeal. You either have it or you're ugly. You either have the undeniable gift of being able to induce a Hurricane Katrina in a lady's skimpies or a North Korean missile in a man's boxer shorts on sight, or, I'm afraid, you're busted. Ugly. Void of sexual capital. Sexually bankrupt. Yuck.

Of course, sex appeal also encompasses power, personality, purse, etc. But for the purpose of this chapter, 'sex appeal' means: is there a long line of people dying to get into your pants or not?

If the answer is yes then you're lucky: studies (by somewhat respectable white people) find that sexually attractive people tend to fare better in their careers.[1]

'Why?' your slowness asketh.

Well, there are many reasons, but there is always likely to be one simple universal truth for the swift career advancement of professionals with a long line of people wishing to get into their underwear: there is a long line of people wishing to get into their underwear.

---

1 According to the University of Essex: 'Forget University! It's a PRETTY FACE that helps guarantee a successful career', *Daily Mail*, 6 December 2013.

Using the remarkably tasteful and accurate words of Bim Adewunmi, that great black British woman of words: your employability is often linked to your 'fuckability'.[2]

You have to use what you have to get what you want. It's natural and logical; it's why you get things like an education and adopt some form of respectability politics. So, if you're oozing sex appeal then you might as well use it to get yourself ahead professionally too.

By the last paragraph, you could be forgiven for thinking that this chapter will suggest you prostitute yourself, mount the metaphorical greasy pole in order to work your way up the other metaphorical greasy professional pole. Well, this chapter doesn't do any such thing – not because it is morally wrong (morality is merely an unnecessary emotional obstacle to achieving professional outcomes) but because it would be counterproductive (more on which to come).

Sexual Politics and Economics Explained

Sex is big business. In fact, it is the biggest business in the world (you could call it 'Big Sex'). For pretty much everyone (above a certain age) is in it. Like freedom and using a toilet at a British railway station, sex is never free. Everyone – yourself included – trades something in order to get fucked. Looks, hard cold cash, power, sanity, soul, time, privacy, respectability, effort in the gym, dieting/skipped meals, half of everything you have spent your life working for – we all trade something for sex. No one fucks for free.

2 'There's an elephant in Harvey Weinstein's hotel room', *BuzzFeed*, 18 October 2017.

THINK LIKE A WHITE MAN

As stated earlier, the immediate key currency of Big Sex is looks. The better you look, the sexually richer you are, the more you can demand from a potential partner … or buyer.

The old-school players were quite scientific on sexual economics and politics. They broke it down as follows:

- A person who sells sex is known as a 'hoe';[3]
- A person who pays for sex is known as a 'trick';[4]
- A person who facilitates the safe and successful sale and solicitation of sex is known as a 'pimp',[5] or a 'dating' app;[6]
- A person who sells sex, receives payment but often doesn't deliver is known as a 'spouse'.[7]

Blade meets jugular; this chapter doesn't advocate the oldest profession in the world: hoe-ing (or 'prostitution'). What this chapter *does* firmly advocate is the second oldest profession in the world: pimping.

With the dishonourable exception of Hollywood, because sexual politics isn't as honest or blatant a trade in the corporate world as it is in, say, Amsterdam's red light district, in the context of professionalism by 'pimping' I mean: 'to ruthlessly exploit the sordid, depraved and sometimes desperate sexual cravings of others – "tricks" (usually white men or White Men) – towards you (or, preferably, towards third parties) to your benefit without yourself being coerced into affirmatively, conclusively and positively responding to a sexual advance'.

3 Julia Roberts in *Pretty Woman*.
4 Richard Gere in *Pretty Woman*.
5 Strangely omitted from *Pretty Woman*.
6 *Pretty Woman* predated the threat of automation.
7 Also strangely omitted from *Pretty Woman*.

In short, you don't want to be the hoe, the trick and certainly not the long-suffering spouse. In order to progress and achieve your goals, you want to be the profiteering facilitator: the pimp.

You want to profit from the milk without owning the cow. (This is called the Uber business model.) You want to get the power and the money without giving up the honey.

Before we dive deeper into the pimping element and how to achieve it, it is critical to understand why having sex, i.e. selling sex or 'hoe-ing' for short, for professional expediency purposes is just not a good idea.

M.I. Yayo!

Miami. If sex was a company Miami would be its global headquarters. And King of Diamonds (KoD) – 50,000 square feet of black-ass-shaking glory – would be its boardroom.[8] There is absolutely nowhere better in the solar system to attain a quality education on sex and sexual politics than the mighty twerk-athon that is this esteemed establishment.

Like the pursuit of getting laid, academic research can at times take you to strange places. It took me to KoD, where I met 'Cece', a twenty-eight-year-old decade-long veteran of working the stripper pole. To conceptualise Cece, think Chimamanda Ngozi Adichie giving her now clichéd anti-cliché TED talk 'The Danger of a Single Story' while thunder-twerking from the top of a forty-foot pole.

Cece was to the human eye what onions in hot cooking oil are to the human nose. She was beauty, confidence, grace and acrobatics personified. Most importantly, Cece was sharp as shit.

8 Which, befittingly, would make the CEO of King of Diamonds, the rapper Akinyele (of 'Put It In Your Mouth' and 'Fuck Me For Free' fame) CEO of Sex Inc.

In a discussion about the shocking 70% drop in her income, she gave me a Harvard-worthy business lesson draped in a prose Soyinka, Shakespeare or Sister Souljah would be proud of:

'The strip club is the most American thing in America. It *is* America. America is a land of dreams and so is the strip club. Big ass, big titties, pretty-ass smiles play the same role in the strip club that bright lights and big cities play in America. It attracts everyone, keeps them here or trying to get here, hoping that one day they, too, may be able to have a slice of the action. But it is a dream, it ain't real. America and the strip club are both built on fuck-niggas fucking niggas over,[9] but they're not really real. An illusion. And the same thing destroying America is the same thing destroying the strip club: greed and corruption.'

She took a long pause.

'Fantasy will keep a nigga like you spending money for hours and coming back for years. Men will do so much for you, to please you, so maybe one day over the rainbow they'll get to sleep with you. With me, it ain't gonna happen. Because when you fuck you'll probably not see that person again – plus I got my girlfriend at home. The old timers who used to own this place knew this and kept the hoes out, the new niggas don't think long term. It has totally messed the business up.'

She paused for a sip of her drink and a puff of weed.

I interjected. 'So the "hoes" are like China or the Mexicans and you're like America?' I asked, wanting to re-trigger her America analogy.

'Shut up, dumb nigga,' she responded with a laugh. Before she could wrap up her story she was summoned back to the stage.

What did we learn from Cece?

9 For the benefit of white people, when Cece says 'fuck-niggas fucking niggas over' she means White Men and other non-desirables exploiting vulnerable people for profit. Or 'capitalism' for short.

1. There are people, most of them women, with the intellectual and social capacity to become CEOs of major corporations dancing on poles in clubs.

2. Teasing pays more than pleasing. Creating fantasy is more rewarding than fulfilling it.

The pertinent point to black professional life is simple: sex sells. But it pays a better dividend in a professional setting when you're not having it. As the old cliché goes: lead the horse to the water, but for the love of an unsullied white woman's tears don't let the horse have sex with you.

Where There Is Monogamy There Is Opportunity

Corporations tend to prefer to hire and promote married people.[10] Particularly married (white) men.[11] Because they'll have more to lose than single people, married people are considered to be more 'stable' and easier to control and extract effort from. They have children, school fees, mortgages, social standing, high standards of living, a couple of holidays a year, a nice car, a pet and so on. If they're lucky, they have someone on the side who they are also trying to keep happy.

10 'Do Married Men Really Get Promoted Fastest?', *Psychology Today*, 20 January 2013. In one of the firms I worked for you were 'encouraged' (unofficial policy) to take a glance at the ring finger of a person being interviewed. Sight of a wedding ring always placed the person in a slightly better standing during the interview.
11 'Marriage Research: being married helps men get promoted, but not women', *HuffPost*, 18 January 2013.

As a result, they're more reliant on the job. They make better corporate slaves.

Nevertheless, these happily married people still have those urges that are present in all humans. They still remain sophisticated base animals with desires that they are actively supressing. Some control their urges, others are controlled by their urges. Some will act on their burning desires, others won't. The key thing is that those urges are there. And to this end, for the black professional with any remote hint of sex appeal (or with a hot 'friend'), this weakness, these desires, need to be ruthlessly exploited. Time to whoop you some tricks.

Bear witness to a few eternal truths:

- Where there is a bakery there is flour.
- Where there are black people there is creativity.
- Where there are white people there is racism.
- Where there is smoke ... there is weed.
- Where there is success there is persistence in the face of failure.
- Where there is monogamy there is hypocrisy, dishonesty and infidelity.

There is no greater indicator of human dishonesty than monogamy.

Monogamy is a man-made structure. A White-Man-made structure to be precise (and almost totally without probable factual merit). It largely complies with property rights and supposedly aids the development and advancement of a stable society, i.e. a society ripe for White Men to take full advantage of. Polygamy, for all the bad publicity it has received in recent millennia, is certainly more natural. But as monogamy is the flavour of the month, man has to deceive both himself and everyone else that he or she only has eyes for their significant other. Laughably untrue, but the game is the game. Man is only really as 'faithful' as his opportunities present. The more he can get away with, the more he'll do.

When you peel the onion layers of a monogamist back, what you'll find is a liar, a bullshitter, a conformer, a people pleaser, a ball of pent-up sexual frustration … an actor portraying a faithful spouse.

Even the most 'I've been happily married for 217 years' white man and White Man alike still have a need to feel desired. To feel sexually relevant outside his or her past-their-sell-by-date partner. So, when that exotic (i.e. dark-skinned) sex bomb in the office starts to show him or her a little extra-curricular attention – the odd flirty eye batting, the saucy joke, the suggestive leaning over at their desk with a micro twerk thrown in for good measure, the slow dance at the Christmas party – it is often more than enough to keep his/her lame old heart racing.

Even if they are ardent, full-blown Make America Great Again cap-wearing white supremacists, the fact that you're black will probably more than blow their mind.[12] Blow their load. And they need that. They need that to keep going. They love their spouses and families and probably (hopefully) won't leave them for you – thank God – but they need that pretty young 'exotic' thing in the office to keep them feeling good about themselves. Keeps that trick feeling like a man or woman.

Rees-Mogg and his ilk may well fly their red, white and blue rags of choice at the little tiki-torch Brexit rally but they will tearfully bow before the mighty revolutionary but

12 'Kara Young, a biracial model who dated Trump, said she "never heard him say a disparaging comment towards any race"', *New York Times*, 17 August 2017.

gangsta red, black and green flag of pan Africanist unity in the bedroom. Racism shuts down on the mattress and reboots on the floor right beside it.

Back to you. You, my black friend, are going to be objectified. Might as well get praised, promoted and paid at the same time. Like a pimp, you want to make the money, but unlike a hoe, you're not willing to sell/have sex (I hope). Take Cece's advice: string them along. Create sexual fantasy but don't fulfil it. Tease but don't please. Whoop that trick.

Beware of Risks

There are, however, risks associated with this strategy that you must be aware of. And must be prepared to curtail.

The key risk associated with stringing a White Man along and creating a sexual fantasy is that said person may get tired of being strung along and may one day demand to know:

'Are you going to fuck me or not?'

This is something you must be prepared for. At this stage, the jig is very much up and you need to decide if fulfilling the sexual fantasy you have created is something you wish to 'honour' or not.

My advice? Have your polite excuses ready and waiting for launch:

- 'I love you ... but as I do my best friend/brother/sister/father/mother';
- 'I fear that making love to you could risk jeopardising our friendship. And that, I'm afraid, is a risk I'm just not willing to take';
- 'I find you immensely attractive but I'm currently celibate for vegan reasons';

- 'I have a burning desire to make love to you, too, but I recently discovered I'm allergic to human genitalia'.

Any of the classic 'gently letting him/her know that it is a HELL, MOTHERFUCKING NO' lines should suffice. If you need more advice on these lines, then it would be prudent to find the most attractive woman or unattractive poor man you can find and they should be able to inform you of a few dozen of them.

Old fools quickly wise up when they realise that they are not about to have their way with you. Tread carefully at this point if dealing with a White Man, for the rejected horny White Man is dangerous. Your refusal to follow him into the bedroom may lead to him fucking you raw and hard in the boardroom.

Beware of Mission Creep

Another risk to note in relation to sex and the workplace is the risk of mission creep: *don't* fall in love. If you're not careful, one second you'll be convincing yourself that you won't fulfil his fantasy, and the next, you'll have your pants round your ankles and poppers up your nostrils talking to yourself about how 'he isn't that bad-looking for eighty-three, White Men age like fine wine ...'

The Story of Melania

In September 1998, Slovenian model Melanija Knavs (who 'whitified' her name to Melania Knauss) attended a party in New York and met an overweight orange White Man called Donald. He asked for her number, but like all self-respecting macks, she took his. Seven years later she became Donald's third wife. Eleven years after that she became America's forty-fifth First Lady.

In eighteen quick years she went from an immigrant so hard up she was hawking naked pictures of herself to the highest bidder to First Lady. Easily the most successful immigration story since Tony Montana received his Green Card for murdering a communist.

Fast-forward to 2019, and no one in their right mind really believes that Melania glances at Donald and purrs with fantasies like 'I can't wait to get him home so I can make sweet passionate love to this precious beautiful man of mine. I'm going to ride him like Barack Obama did the black community tonight.'

Of course not. The First Lady isn't mad. She's thinking, 'I can't wait till this orange thing dies. I'll have a five-year struggle with his stupid kids then I'll take all the money back to the caves of Slovenia. I'll be free. Free from Donald. Hallelujah.'

She may pose like America's First Lady but she is really America's First Pimp. She is biding her time.

Final point, as the fantastically unattractive, unappealing and devoid of sexual capital former Secretary of State Henry Kissinger once said, 'Power is the ultimate aphrodisiac.' He should know.

Black professionals might want to remember those wise words when the power is in your hands, for you, too, will one day be a thirsty old fool. The direction of travel is one-way.

In conclusion: somewhere in the world right now there is a black professional on his knees with a White Man's penis in his mouth trying to suck favour, prominence and riches out of it. Don't be that person. You really don't want to be that person.

However, you do want to find your way to make hay out of that person's 'efforts'.

Always remember: you're a teaser and not a pleaser. A pimp and not a prostitute. An exploiter and never the exploited.

187 Quick Dos and Don'ts: 138–154

138. Do note that learning from your mistakes is a privilege, one not often afforded to black professionals.

139. Do associate yourself with whatever or whoever is popular right now. Yes, dick-riding is a less than perfect form of transportation but it's a cold world. You have to stay near the heat in order to keep warm.

140. Don't be deterred by the fact that white people take other white people's word as paramount over yours. In the eyes of white people, the White Man's ice is colder.

141. Don't be deterred by the fact that black people take white people's word as paramount over yours. In the eyes of black people, the White Man's ice is colder.

142. Do partake in public sympathising with white inconvenience while ignoring black plague, death and terrible suffering.

143. Do note the Whytelaw rules for assisted corporate elevation:

- White Men get sponsors;
- White people and white men get mentors;
- White Tragedies get coaches;
- Black people get glossy diversity reports.

144. Don't ever admit to any of the following being your favourite film: *Scarface, Menace II Society, Bullet Boy, Adulthood, Boyz n the Hood, Baby Boy, Django Unchained* and, especially, *Bamboozled*.

145. Do watch Spike Lee's *Bamboozled* (especially if you're a creative).

146. Do consider becoming an academic if your professional career stalls. Academia is possibly the only arena in which you can be paid well and afforded widespread respectability for essentially being a well-informed and therefore pissed-off black person.

147. Don't mistake the company's rivals for your personal rivals. You'll probably join them one day.

148. Don't wait for perfect weather to sow seed. Create opportunities for yourself daily.

149. Don't be afraid to ask for what you want in exchange for whatever lucrative tip or connection you can offer the company. For example, work in oil and gas and have a powerful cousin in 'Pipelineria'? Well, demand a huge pay rise, a board-level promotion, two kilos per month of the latest popular narcotic and significantly reduced working hours in exchange for an introduction. Or take an even more demanding offer to the company's rivals.

150. Do 'pass' for white if you're light-skinned enough. It will work wonders for your career and quality of life. Seek therapy to ensure you don't go too deep with your cover.

151. Do talk up the few drops of European blood that may run through your veins ('I'm 0.025% Irish, Australian and white South African') but never mention the pitch-black genitals you popped out of.

152. Do find solace in the wise non-genocidal words of Madeleine Albright: 'There's plenty of room in the world for mediocre men, but there is no room for mediocre women.' Draw motivation (or succumb to depression) from the fact that there is no room for mediocre black people regardless of how much sensitive flesh hangs between your legs.

153. Do mourn like your own mother was just murdered (by a white policeman) if a wild animal is killed. In fact, if you ever find yourself at the funeral of, say, a rhinoceros, then, if opportunity presents itself, throw yourself on the coffin as it is being lowered into the ground in a bundle of tears and emotion.

154. Do remind yourself every morning that no black person ever went broke telling white people exactly what they want to hear. Then get up, get out and go find a white person to lie to.

CHAPTER 13

You Need a Mentor (or Two)

'Experto credite.'
Latin and therefore respectable and intellectually
unquestionable for: *'Trust one who has gone through it.'*

– Virgil (the Roman poet, not the Million Dollar Man
Ted DiBiase's black butler)

No man is an island unto himself. No idea is original and the same goes for mistakes. According to Socrates, 'the only true wisdom is knowing you know nothing'. A 'secret' job opening is only a secret until you know about it. How your company works in practice will pretty much be a semi-mystery until someone pulls the curtain back for you.

For the reasons listed above, and many more, you need a mentor.

From the wisest, oldest and foremost criminal mafia boss to the leader of the free world (roles which are not entirely mutually exclusive), everyone needs someone. And that is especially true for the black professional.

Theoretically, a mentor serves as an adviser, a motivator and a confidant. Theoretically, a mentor can help you to navigate the politics of the firm, advise you on difficult situations, provide very good career progression advice, make you an insider, help with the promotions process, keep your boss in check, and show you the skills to help you do your job better. Theoretically, a mentor is a great idea.

The same is true in practice, but choosing a mentor is a critical subject that requires one to tread carefully.

The first element to choosing a mentor is, well, choosing a mentor. You have to make sure *you* choose your mentor yourself.

Some companies will take the liberty of assigning mentors to employees. They'll probably consider it a favour. Wisdom advises against this, as it's not really in your interest. The results of company-imposed mentoring relationships are often similar to the results permeating from forced marriages: it will feel awkward from the outset; it could work but the likelihood is it probably won't. And therefore, it will probably end in acrimony (possibly with the corporate equivalent of an 'honour' killing).

Plus, if the firm chooses your mentor for you, there is a good chance that said person is not really a mentor at all. There is a good chance that he is a slave catcher or police officer (some would argue that the latter two roles have quite a lot in common) of some sort, a means of keeping you on a close leash while making you feel good (but actually working for the man, the White Man).

You have to trust your mentor, trust their advice and feel comfortable confiding in them. So, returning to the relationship metaphor, you have to choose your mentor in the same way you'd choose your wife or husband. Friends, family or, in this instance, the company may set you up on a blind date, but ultimately you have to ensure it is you doing the choosing. And you have to live with the decision.

Qualities matter in your mentor. Your mentor has to be

someone who is respected in the business, respected by you, senior, successful, experienced, savvy and likeable.

Your mentor has to be someone who is going to 'do something' for you, who is going to help to propel you. Their position and attributes are critical but they have to be willing to use them for your benefit. In short, you need your mentor to also be your sponsor. Someone who can vouch for the fact that you're worth the time, investment and 'risk' (a word that is bandied about lavishly when it comes to black professionals).

If they tick all of these boxes, all they'll need to do is whisper the words, 'I think young Cassandra is ready to move up to the next level. It would be a crying shame to lose her to a rival firm.'

And faster than you can say '55% of white women voted for a racist male chauvinist pig over a fellow white woman in the 2016 US presidential election' young Cassandra has been promoted. Why? Because young Cassandra's boss wants to look good in the eyes of young Cassandra's mentor.

If this was a conventional self-help book, i.e. written for and by white people, this chapter would have ended at the paragraph above. But, of course, for the black professional there are added complications.

While everyone needs a mentor, the black professional needs at least two. You guessed it: a white one and a black one. Ebony and ivory. A négroïde and a caucasoïde. Chocolate and pork. This is not borne out of spite or a desire to be evil, it is borne out of reality, realpolitik and necessity.

The White Mentor

Starting with the white mentor: why does a black professional explicitly need a white mentor? Why does a member of an oppressed group need to be mentored by a member of their oppressor group?

The great African–American soul singer James Brown, one of the all-time blackest of men, once sang that 'It's A Man's Man's Man's World'. A heartfelt song (which was ironically penned by superwoman Betty Jean Newsome) delivered with great depth, passion and soul, it should come as less than shocking news to learn that the title is only partially correct.

We do indeed live in a man's world, but not any man's world. This is firmly a white man's world. *The* White Man's world to be precise. In fact, it is much more of a white woman's world than it is a black person's world. After all, white women, on average, earn and control more wealth than black people of all genders.[1]

Always remember the Mario Van Peebles golden rule: 'who controls the gold, controls the rules.'

On a micro and macro level, white people hold the gold (and the guns) and therefore dictate the rules, call the shots and define the dictionary. That is just the way it is in the world today and this is the way it is almost certainly going to be in your company.

Therefore, choosing a mentor (who meets the qualities listed above) from the 'natural' power pool is just common sense. It is good strategy.

There is another lesser spoken reason why having a white mentor is a good idea. And it goes a little something like this: *Cry Freedom*, *Amistad*, *Blood Diamond*, *Dangerous Minds*, *The Help*, *Mississippi Burning*, *To Kill a Mockingbird*, *Blind Side*, *Free State of Jones*, *Machine Gun Preacher*, *Indiana Jones and the Temple of Doom*, *Lincoln*, etc.

---

1 'The workforce is even more divided by race than you think', *The Atlantic*, 6 November 2013.

What do all of these hit movies have in common?

Simple. They are all white saviour films. Films in which white people come to the rescue of black (and other non-white people but usually black) people. Even though 99% of the time they are saving black people from other white people – bad white people. Either that, or they are saving black people from systems that are in place for the benefit of white people – both good and bad white people.

The white saviour movie genre didn't pop out of the clear blue sky. It reflects the collective thinking and practices of white people. To be fair, this is not true of all white people.

Key themes:

- Save someone or a few people as opposed to eradicating the system that is holding them captive or subjugated principally to your benefit. And feel good.

- Donate a dozen peppercorns a month to save this kwashiorkor-riddled African baby but maintain the economic and political system that permits you to benefit from his suffering firmly intact. And feel good.

- Sing 'Do They Know It's Christmas?'. And feel good.

Not convinced? Our dear white people are being unfairly tarred as a monolithic collective? Want definitive proof? Want to test the hypothesis? Take a slight detour and conduct the Whytelaw White Justice and Compassion Experiment. Follow the steps below.

The Whytelaw White Justice and Compassion Experiment

Step 1. Gather together no less than twenty of the loveliest, anti-racist, anti-inequality, latte-sipping nice white people you can find ('subjects' henceforth);

Step 2. Ask subjects if they believe slavery and colonialism were wrong, criminal and the building blocks of white wealth and black poverty. Remove subjects who respond negatively.

Step 3. Ask subjects if they are in favour of repairing the clear damage done to black people. Do not, however, use the word 'reparations'. Remove subjects who respond negatively.

Step 4. Ask subjects if they are willing to repair this damage done to black people by paying reparations (at the government level, hence more taxes and less latte) for slavery, colonialism, Jim Crow, segregation, the prison industrial complex, the Rolling Stones, Justin Bieber and other ills that have plagued the lives of black people largely to the benefit of white people. Inform them that this would arguably make the world much more equal very quickly. Remove subjects who respond negatively.

Step 5. You'll quickly realise that your subjects are quite comfortable with the status quo and not quite so 'anti-inequality' as they proclaimed themselves to be as you recline and relax in the empty room.[2]

Conclusion: Equality has much in common with the suburbs of Paris: white folk may say nice things about it but they DO NOT want to go there. *Mais non!*

2 'Overwhelming opposition to reparations for slavery and Jim Crow', Yougov, 2 June 2014.

THINK LIKE A WHITE MAN

Consistent with the white saviour mentality there's a good chance that your white mentor will treat you like someone they are rescuing (think Sandra Bullock in *The Blind Side* or Bob Geldof shoving a sugar-free biscuit into a starving child's mouth in one of his never-ending and never fruitful Africa crusades). They may wish to treat you as a child they are raising rather than a grown professional. Either way, provided they are sprinkling their star dust on you and working to help elevate you, you're in the money. A win is a win.

Regardless of whether they are treating you as a mentee or a baby, it would be wise to ensure that you do not create the impression of helplessness. No one respects a seemingly helpless person. If people see you working to push yourself forward they'll be more inclined to help you.

The game ain't based on sympathy.

Let them play Skeeter,[3] Louanne Johnson,[4] or the fruitcake *Kony 2012* white boy who lost his mind and ran through the street naked[5] all they want. Watch, listen, learn and absorb as much as possible from them. A white mentor or a naked white saviour is still a mentor, still a good person, and their time should be valued and efforts appreciated. Even if the road to black hell is paved with the good intentions of these very people.

The Black Mentor

The white mentor can only advise you on so much. A white person may struggle to understand how best to keep a black person motivated (i.e. a black person not enslaved by them)

3 Emma Stone's character in *The Help*.
4 Michelle Pfeiffer's white saviour/teacher character in *Dangerous Minds*.
5 'Kony 2012: Jason Russell's Naked Meltdown, TMZ': https://www.youtube.com/watch?v=yGiR2TmeNYc.

because they may struggle to fully comprehend the motivations – both explicit and implicit – of a black person. They haven't lived the experience, haven't carried the cross and aren't socialised in that manner. They are not about that life.

There is only so much a black person can wisely confide in a white person in a corporate setting. For example, it would be foolish to inform your white mentor that you suspect your boss, one of the most senior and respected people in the business, is an out-and-out-shaking-it-all-about white supremacist.

Your white mentor can't give what they don't have. Asking them to advise you on issues that are specific to a black professional is like a thirteen-year-old girl asking her four-year-old brother for advice on period pains. Laughably futile.

And this is what makes a black mentor a necessity.

Your black mentor, like your white mentor, should have all the attributes a good mentor needs. They need to be knowledgeable, respected by you, respected by the business and so forth. However, an additional, somewhat unique yet quintessential quality that must be sought in a black mentor is age.

Your black mentor needs some age on them. The wisdom, knowledge, understanding, frustration, pessimism and realness that usually comes with age in black skin is something that every black professional needs to learn from.

There is a clear inverse relationship between growing older as a black person and caring increasingly less for the rat race and racial social order that comes with being a black professional.

In sweet and short terms, the older black professional usually doesn't give a fuck any more. Say the wrong thing to them and you will be served with an ass-whupping they've been soaking in the sour milk of the civil rights struggle since the 60s.

They have seen it all: racism, favouritism, overlooked promotions and more. And at a certain point, God, Ogun, or whatever your belief system or lack thereof is, does indeed grant you the serenity to accept things you just cannot change. They, the older black professionals, are at that age when politeness, politics and etiquette have long been booted out the window. And they will tell it to you 100% as it is. They will keep it real and raw. Think latterday Darcus Howe, Paul Mooney, Donna Brazile, Monique and Diane Abbott.[6] You're one slick comment away from a five-finger Toxteth special slap round your face.

Please note: you want your black mentor to be an elder, not just old. You want the likes of Sir Sidney Poitier and Dame Shirley Bassey, not Bunny and Uncle Ruckus (or pastors Mark Burns and Darrell Scott). Kofi Annan, not Koko B. Ware.

Another thing you need to understand and appreciate in your black mentor is that he or she may not have the power and leverage that your white mentor does. Your white mentor is from the white power pool; your black mentor is not. That doesn't mean that they won't be powerful; they may indeed be. It means that their power isn't naturally backed up by the dominant, heavily connected component of society, i.e. white people. Regardless of how powerful they may be, they, too, are trying to keep their heads above water. And if they go too far (become too black) they may face ruin.

In addition to all of the things that your white mentor does for you, your black mentor remains critical for the following additional crucial reasons:

1. They should be able to help you better understand and navigate the latent racial politics within the company.

2. They should be someone who understands where you're coming from and is therefore able to tailor their mentoring to suit your specific needs.

6 One of the most racially insulted people on the face of the earth.

3. You should be able to learn from their specific mistakes and the difficulties they have faced as their experience may not be entirely different to yours.

4. They should be able to explain in raw terms who is who within the organisation, and how such people are likely to behave and view you. Specifically, they should be able to separate the subconscious racist idiot, the UKIP-voting, Trump-loving white supremacist mastermind and the conscious anti-racist allies from each other. Separate the white man from the White Man. The chump from the Trump.

5. Like your white mentor, they should be able to read between the lines for you and offer interpretations. What is your boss really up to? Is the department treating you fairly? Are you deemed talent or just a worker? Is your remuneration an inside joke? Based on a set of actions, is your boss racist? These are all questions your black mentor should be able to nail for you.

6. You should be able to confide totally, yet sensibly, in your black mentor.

7. Your black mentor will be your black man (or woman) in a grey suit. They should be able to tell you when the game is up. When it is time to just throw in the towel, give up and go elsewhere. This is always a hard message for anyone to receive and accept. For a black person it is even harder to receive from a white person, given the historical baggage, social connotations and, therefore, the healthy distrust you (should) have of white people.

8. Finally, they should be able to tell you, discreetly, whether your white mentor is worth the time of day.

As normal, social order rules apply. Black people congregating in larger numbers than usual in white spaces often induces fear and panic (it makes white people think of enslaved Africans planning a rebellion or Crips and Bloods uniting to fight white supremacy). So, your relationship with your black mentor might not be as conventional as your relationship with your white one. In fact, it may be incognito, or you may just have to find a black mentor external to the organisation altogether (admittedly less than ideal, but not useless).

'Winston Russell'

My black mentor, Winston Russell, was a gentleman of Jamaican descent. He was born and raised there but completed his tertiary studies at one of the elite British institutions.[7] His Jamaican accent had somehow woven into a posh British one that made him sound 'exotic' (to use white people parlance) yet was grandiose enough to be who he was and where he was: a black man in a deeply elitist white company.

He was always immaculately dressed. His grey hairs added to his distinguished appearance. He had that look that motivates grandmothers to get back in the gym.

In public, Winston was as loveable as Dr Cliff Huxtable in the 80s (long before the man who played Dr Cliff was actually convicted of sexual assault), but behind closed doors – black closed doors, that is – he laid it down. He did not bite his

---

7 One of the many benefits of the Cold War being that white people and Hollywood villain white people bidded for black affection by opening their elite academic institutions to them.

tongue, suffer fools or fail to empty his cartridge. He told it as it was.

In fact, much of this book comprises lessons learned from my black mentor. I would have called it *Dreams from My Mentor* but that sounds strangely familiar.

Winston knew what he was worth and he knew he wasn't getting it. He knew that if he was the right side of pale he'd have become a lot richer and had a more rewarding career. As a result, he was bitter and angry. But like a Mary J. Blige quiet storm record he was dignified with it. He clearly had regrets but he had learned how to live with them.

My mentoring relationship with Winston was more of a friendship in nature. It wasn't formal at all. But he knew I was soaking up game from him. He knew that I relied on him for advice. He knew I needed him.

It began with simple tips. 'What are you doing wearing black shoes and a brown belt? Don't you know how to dress properly? Who the hell raised you?' he would ask jokingly.

Another time, when he saw me going home as my colleagues were going for drinks, he said, 'If you want to get to the top, you have to be an insider. If you don't go to the social events, you'll always be on the outside. That's where careers are built – in the pub and at the dinner party. There is no diversity scheme at the pub.'

Eventually I invited him out to lunch.

When we finally got down to it, Winston immediately went from magic negro to Marcus Mosiah Garvey. From Uma Thurman to Umar Johnson. The usual Richard Curtis-style white-friendly jokes were nowhere to be found. It felt that little bit more relaxed. The tone of his laughter was different – more honest – his voice less posh – a little more grit (a lickle more yardie). By the time the drinks arrived, it felt like I'd known Winston all my life. So I felt I could ask him about his biggest career regret.

After rambling on about finding a good woman and starting a family for a bit, he launched into a conversation that changed my life – one that radicalised me ...[8]

8 Sans the stuff that makes you want to fly a plane into a building or drive a car into an anti-racism rally.

CHAPTER 14

Believe in Yourself

*'I'm asking you to believe – not in my ability to
create change, but in yours.'*

– Barack Obama

Winston's next stream of consciousness contained the most important piece of advice I'd ever been given. Surprisingly, it wasn't 'Kill whitey NOW!'.

With intense concentration, Winston began …

'Where do you get your hair cut?'

'Shaun's on Walworth Road. Or D&L in Holloway,' I responded.

'Why don't you just pop into Toni & Guy to get your trim? Slick operation and they're everywhere.'

'Absurd,' I said in a fit of hysterics. 'They wouldn't know what to do with my hair and would just mess it up. They'd probably put foil and stuff on my hairline.'

'So you wouldn't trust a white institution with your hairline but you'd trust one with your career, pension and decades of your life?'

I was reduced to silence.

'Boulé, don't be me. Believe in yourself. Believe in your own genius. Harness your ideas and start a business of your own. If you're smart enough and dedicated enough to work here and climb the ladder, you're smart enough to work here, climb the ladder and build your own business at the same time.'

I found Winston's words to be fascinating, forthright, but still somewhat laughable. Here was my experienced and esteemed corporate chocolate par excellence mentor telling me to circumvent the stumbling blocks that most black professionals face by building a business of my own. In the limited spare time I had outside the business. At that moment, it sounded completely asinine to my young ears.

He continued: 'In a capitalist society or a racist society that happens to be capitalist, or the other way round, capitalism is the game. And you're either in the game or you're getting fucked.'

'These organisations will suck you dry and spit you out. And if anything happens to you, they'll move on quickly. Not taking risks on yourself is not worth the risk.'

'Things are changing now though, Winston. Companies are becoming more—'

'Slick,' he jumped in. 'They're becoming better at hiding their crap. Word to the wise: I hope it's sufficient.'

He called for the bill and paid for it.

'Look. Solve a problem. Fulfil a need. Supply a demand. Start small, start slowly, start alone or start with friends, but make sure you start – that's what matters. And make sure you keep going. You'll make mistakes, you'll lose money, you'll lose your temper, but don't lose your patience and determination, and in the long term you won't regret it. You'll be smiling because you'll be free and happy.'

Winston stood up, finished his drink and wrapped up our conversation. 'One last thing, Boulé: man, striped shirts and striped ties don't go together. Bushmen like you are ruining it for all of us!' He shook my hand and then grabbed me into a hug.

'Good luck, Boulé.' And that was the last I saw of Winston. Days later, the company revealed that he had developed a very serious illness ... as they were announcing that his job was up for grabs.

I didn't think much of Winston's cover of the Michael Jackson classic 'Wanna Be Startin' Somethin'' for a few years. In fact, I thought it was faintly ludicrous at first. But as months became years and with years came tears, it was made very clear to me in successive firms that Winston was right.

The Story of Us

From affirmative action employers in the US to so-called 'equal opportunity' employers in the UK, there is no escaping the black experience in the corporate structure.

Racism. Double standards. Slower, lack of or no career progression. Enormous pay discrepancies. Greater effort for much less reward. Micro-aggressions. Macro-aggressions. Proverbial nuclear aggressions. White masks. Last in, first out.

There is barely any comparative upside to being black in the white corporate world (other than getting paid and, perhaps, interracial lovemaking, should you be into that sort of thing).

The stigma of blackness is total in corporate environments.

We suffer, we smile, we betray everything we are and love, and then we suddenly fall sick and die before we can claim our pensions. And yes, we pick up thirty pieces of silver a month, but, unlike Judas, we're usually not even selling out a self-important third party: we're selling ourselves out.

We can do much better.

There is only so long a people can stomach something before enough is finally enough. There is only so long we can continue to repeat this cycle. To be fair, 'only so long' is quite long when you have a mortgage, school fees, a side piece, etc. to keep paying for.

White supremacy is like oxygen or Adele's next single: it's everywhere. You can't really escape it. You can only manage its flare-ups. Like eczema. In order to minimise the risk of failure – of white supremacy finally breaking me – I had to branch out on my own. I had to take some risks. I had to bet on myself, my ability. And in order to do that I had to believe in myself. It was time for me to build.

This book will not detail the exact nature of the business I went into, however, please rest assured that your purchase of this book made happy reading for my accountant (and a slew of other white people banking on this becoming a success). And if you didn't purchase it, then fuck you.

As opposed to 'working twice as hard' (and everything else that the black professional experience entails), work just as hard as anyone else – put in the effort and hope for the best, but prepare for the worst by founding and finessing your own establishment.

There are, of course, risks associated with establishing a business, but for a black professional, indeed a black person, the risk of not doing so is possibly even more significant.

Want to fight racism? Build a business.

Want to go to your grave a happy and accomplished black person? Build a business.

Want to minimise the risk of failure as a black professional in the white corporate world? Build a business.

Want to be as black as you want? Build a business. (Or move to Uganda.)

Institutional racism, in fact even racism of the Kramer calibre ('HE'S A NIGGER, HE'S A NIGGER!'),[1] becomes a lot less

1 'Seinfeld actor lets fly with racist tirade', *The Guardian*, 22 November 2006.

potent when you have reduced the one thing that grants it its potency: power. Especially economic power.

The N-word, white supremacy, white privilege and even country music lose their devastating sting when you've castrated them by nurturing, harnessing and working on your own ideas to build and, if need be, rebuild your own business.

The more you work on your own ideas outside the corporation, the less likely it is that you'll worry about everything and anything that could possibly be thrown at you by the corporate world. The more fuck-off money you have, the easier it is to tell them to fuck off. (Although managing relationships is a smart thing to do so you may want to chill out on telling 'them' to fuck off.) In fact, it may even serve as a form of comfort or therapy (in place of excessive alcohol or food consumption, punishing exercise regimes, religious extremism, emo-blogging, Drake records, etc.).

Believe in yourself. You can do it all by yourself. Lean out. As the alarmingly skinny freedom fighter and committed anti-black racist Mahatma Gandhi once said, 'Be the change you want to see.'

155. Do know your overrated yet sacredly revered White Men. And master the art of pretending to love and revere them. Tony Blair? 'Regardless of his minor missteps, best thing to happen to the Middle East since hummus was discovered.' Boris Johnson? 'Beacon of virtue and honesty.' Justin Bieber? 'The B in R&B.' Cecil Rhodes? 'Unrivalled philanthropist, pinnacle of humanity, diversity champion.' And so on …

156. Do tone down your love of legitimately white yet somehow black people. Of course you love Jon B, Bobby Caldwell, Phil Collins, Teena Marie and Lisa Stansfield, but keep it deep in your black soul.

157. Don't hesitate to strengthen the company alumni when you're in power. Anyone you remotely suspect of causing you problems or, even worse, mounting a challenge to your authority, should swiftly become an unemployment statistic.

158. Do beware of anyone who wants to meet you on a Friday afternoon. That sly bastard probably wants to give you bad news and enough space to get over it, i.e. your precious weekend.

159. 'Do something!' – the magic words that are often followed by a storm of bombs, bullets and mass death when uttered from the lips of enough white people. The moment you hear those words uttered in relation to a country (or even a region) that you're in, immediately, without a second's hesitation, leave.

160. Do beware of any form of stay-in-your-place-ism. And stay-in-your-place-ists.

161. Do note the direction of white flight. Whichever area middle-class white professionals are moving into is an area that you should immediately also move to or buy property in. Such an area will inevitably be better resourced, better protected and offer you greater life opportunities than its 'more diverse' neighbouring areas.

162. Do expect to have the police called on you for any old reason should you follow the point above. In fact, even if white people move in to your neighbourhood en masse, expect to have the police called on you.

163. Do be encouraged by the fact that you can get a lot done if you don't mind which mediocre white man takes credit for it.

164. Do remember the three corporate purposes of a mediocre white man on any project: to trash it, to terminate it, or to take credit for it.

165. Do note that the more mediocre the white man, the louder he screams 'merit'.

166. Don't be shocked when another black person is rolled out to checkmate you during difficult situations. And don't be shocked if you're used for the exact same purpose against another black person.

167. Do drench yourself in jingoism, especially in relation to the armed forces whom you must affectionately refer to as '*our* troops', '*our* boys and girls', '*our* service men and women'. 'God bless *our* troops for keeping *us* safe by going around the world and needlessly bombing the shit out of *them* and *their troops*. And therefore creating determined enemies for *us*.' 'And God bless the White Men who send them to do it.'

168. Do note that a 'charity' is just a form of company. If you work (not volunteer) for one, ensure that you're paid handsomely. The CEO certainly ensures that he or she is. Hundreds of years of 'free' labour is more than enough of a charitable contribution.

169. Do marry well. Marrying well doesn't necessarily mean 'marrying white', however, given how the White Man has structured society, there is significant overlap. Please note that marrying well via marrying white is null and absolutely void if you're marrying a White Tragedy.

170. Do bear in mind that claiming to be socialist in a capitalist corporate structure is like wearing an 'I'M CELIBATE' T-shirt to a Roman orgy.

171. Do beware of any company with any of the Whytelaw Indicators for FSCs (Full of Shit Companies):

- Bring your dog to work day
- Furniture made of vintage cars
- Table football
- Bean bags
- A Conservative politician on the board
- Free breakfast
- A company anthem/song
- Regular free alcohol
- Diversity day

Power: How to Use, Abuse and Retain It

*'Power is the ability to define phenomena and make
it act in a desired manner.'*

— Dr Huey P. Newton (according to some brother on a Rick Ross album)

 few questions (for your big bad corporate self) that
require answers:

- Do white people agree with you even on subjects that
  they normally would not? ('Yes, I agree. Now is not the time
  for reparations debates or discussions. Now is the time for
  negotiations, settlement and immediate payment.')

- Do white people turn bright pink (especially around the
  neck area), sweaty and inarticulate when trying to politely
  oppose your point of view?

- Do white people perform 'deep' interest when asking
  needless questions about your weekend, upcoming holidays, your tastes in music you know they care little for
  (grime, etc.) and so on when you're in a lift with them?

- Do white people practise white-on-white one-upmanship
  in a bid to curry favour with you?

- Do white people treat you like a White Man (or at least a
  white person)?

If the answer is a resounding yes to all of these questions, congratulations, you're either in power or swiftly rising to power. If the answer is a definitive no, condolences, you've still got a lot of shucking and jiving, scheming and conniving to do.

Assuming your answer is yes, then you've been through the storm, survived the drought, camelled through the desert and quenched your thirst.

You're Mammy in *Gone with the Wind* (but unlike Hattie McDaniel you're able to attend the premiere of your own film and write your own Oscar-winning speech). You're a topless Stormzy singing in the rain at the usually all-white-on-the-night Brit Awards. You're Meghan Markle on her second wedding night.

My negus, you've achieved whiteness.

You've manoeuvred through the politics and attained that one elusive thing that stops black excellence from fulfilling its promise: the trust, reverence and confidence of white people.

Far from fighting the powers that be, your black ass is the white powers that be. You've somehow made white supremacy go black.

BUT WAIT! There are a few final questions you need to carefully and affirmatively answer in order to determine if you really have power:

- Are radical black academics and the chattering classes perpetually upset with you and demanding you do more to help black people?

- Do 'normal' black people (i.e. black people who are not radical academics or chattering types) treat your every word like Gospel and basically act like a carnival is in town whenever they see you?

- Are white people trying to take your power and success away from you?

If the answer to these questions is 'HELL, YES!', then further congratulations are due: you really have made it. You really have achieved whiteness.

Nevertheless, beware: the harder you work to make your money and attain your power the harder someone somewhere is working to take it away from you. And in the case of your money, it is often a white lawyer, accountant or private eye acting on behalf of a disgruntled ex-spouse.

Maintaining power is just as tricky a task as attaining it. Maintaining the trust, confidence and reverence of white people is trickier than a black person attaining gainful employment behind the scenes in black music.

Don't believe Dr Whyte? Ask Barack Obama. In the middle of his second term (and as the Black Lives Matter movement was making summer hotter than it had been since Dr King turned up the heat in the 60s), his approval rating for non-college-educated white Americans stood at 27%. When adjusted for sparsely literate, cattle-class white tragedies (i.e. for college-educated white people only) it stood at 42%,[1] while his approval rating among the mothers and fathers of earth – black people (a group he barely lifted a finger to help) – stood at around 84%.[2]

'So, Houdini, how does the magic work?' I hear you ask. How does one maintain the trust and reverence of white people? How does a black professional with real power retain it?

First of all, you'll need some hard-working dreamers around you. People committed to the job and determined to make something of it and by extension themselves.

The key point is that they are easy to manage, hard-working and accepting of their position in life but hopeful for a better

1 http://www.gallup.com/poll/179753/obama-approval-drops-among-working-class-whites.aspx.
2 http://www.gallup.com/poll/180176/blacks-approval-president-obama-remains-high.aspx.

tomorrow. These are workers in the vein of MC Ren and DJ Yella of NWA B-team fame or Tiffany and Eric of Trump youth B-team fame. Someone has to do the boring work and end up anonymous, making blue movies or defending their fascist dad on Twitter.

Occasionally promoting the odd worker on a time-served or undeniably exceptional performance basis is a good tactic for controlling the rest of them and giving them something to dream towards. Keep them working harder. Jumping higher.

Second, in order to maintain power, your core team, your leadership team, must be carefully selected. Getting this right is critical, because, metaphorically speaking – I hope, anyway – one of these people will be standing over your cold dead body with a hot gun in his hand and a sweet smile on his face when the time is right. These are, like you, bloodthirsty sharks. Don't half-step with them, for they will not half-step with you.

They will give you the impression that you are their idol, but do not ever forget for a second that in their coldest and quietest moments they view you as nothing other than a competitor. You're just some person standing in the way of their dream life. You're nothing special to them. You're a piece of unseasoned meat. You are to them what they are to you: disposable.

You must surround yourself with thoroughly competent, ethical, good-hearted, intellectually sound but completely flawed and insecure people. Exploiting these qualities, especially their flaws and insecurities, is absolutely critical. The best way of keeping them from emerging as a threat to your hegemony is to keep them at each other's throats. As was stated earlier on in this book, a divided people are a conquered people. For a corporate leader, a divided leadership team is peace of mind.

As you are now the master of the universe, everyone is your minion. Your pawn. You must know how to treat them. You must use every corporate tool at your disposal – compensation, promotion, commendation, referrals – and use them sparingly and strategically.

In addition to the corporate tools at your disposal, you should also take advantage of the general qualities associated with power. People want powerful people to sprinkle stardust on them. They want to be seen to be close to power in order to attain greater power and influence in the eyes of their peers and rivals. So, who you go to coffee with, spend time laughing with, and occasionally do dinner with, is critical.

A wise person would use these levers strategically. Ration them and, like any self-respecting colonial governor-general, favour one person or group of people today at the expense of another. Then favour the others at a later date. Mind games are critical. They foster competition, efficiency and rivalry. And the occasional revolutionary uprising.

On your route to power, or once you have attained it, some people will reveal themselves to be uncomfortable with the world order as defined by you. Unable to adjust to the new reality. They may even feel emboldened enough to mount a challenge.

In such situations, or even when there is the remotest hint of suspicion that they might step to you, the Quentin Tarantino film *Django Unchained* serves as a great metaphor. There is a scene in the third act when Django – a once enslaved African in America turned bounty hunter – has been captured and sold back into brutal slavery by Stephen, a wretched 'black conservative' (think a fictionalised version of Shaun Bailey but much more likeable and with much better looks). In order to reliberate himself, Django sweet-talks his new captors (some bizarre-sounding white men)[3] and convinces them that he is not a slave.

3 It's unclear whether they are Australian or South African: a moot point as well as a stroke of marketing genius. White Australia and white South Africa are pretty much as bad as each other when it comes to the treatment of black people, they sound fairly similar to the lazy ear and they are both key film distribution markets.

Once he has convinced them that he is but a bounty hunter who can lead them to a large amount of money, they unchain him and hand him a gun. Without hesitation, the split second that the gun lands in Django's hands is the split second all three of them meet their makers.

Django's actions here can be treated as a metaphor for how potential rivals must be dealt with. You must treat any potential blowhard or undermining son of a three-legged, Mike Pence-idolising bitch in the exact same way. The very moment you attain power is the very moment he or she should bolster the company alumni. Do not trifle with them for they will not trifle with you.

Take Stan O'Neal, former Merrill Lynch CEO and perhaps the most senior black professional ever in Wall Street history. The very moment he touched power was the very moment he saw to it that the person most likely to rival him, Thomas H. Patrick, his second-in-command and the man who had helped him rise to power, was shown the exit. Avert a clear problem before it has time to become one.

Evoke the Bush doctrine: always take a pre-emptive strike against those who you suspect may soon strike against you. Fair enough, you may destabilise the entire planet in the process, but if it's good for the White Man, it's good for you.

Kill the germs before they breed and kill you.

But What About Black People?

You're now a black person with power, therefore most black people will see black Santa Claus in your eyes, a wise few will view you like pretty much any other boss and play the game with you like they would anyone else, while the critically intelligent ones will catch the undeniable whiff of sulphuric acid that is synonymous with the devil whenever you're nearby.

Handling black people as a powerful black person in a corporate setting without alienating white people is not easy at all. Certainly not for the faint-hearted. Here are a few tips on how to do it:

1. Identify with the acceptable yet risqué form of black popular culture of the day. Memorise a few of the more stomachable acts and proclaim them to be your favourites.

2. Identify the one worthy 'diversity legend' or political pastor or full-time activist and use the corporate levers to either empower said person or indirectly place them on the payroll. Make sure you have full control of said person and said person knows their role well.[4]

3. In speeches or articles, cautiously evoke the memory or words of Dr Martin Luther King Jnr, Nelson Mandela (but never *ever* Winnie), Usain Bolt (if you must veer into the yardie), Maya Angelou, Oprah Winfrey or prominent black heroes who white people now consider 'safe'.

4. Evoke the words 'community', 'family' and 'brethren', and perhaps even the 'beloved', as often as possible when addressing an exclusively black audience.

5. Insert a little ethnic flair when addressing an exclusively black audience, for example, tell black jokes, speak in Ebonics, wear a little Kente or Ankara, pass Courvoisier round the room, etc.

6. Offer your support on the usual white-perpetrated, black-related outrages (e.g. white policemen killing black people, including children, that sort of thing) that

4 'Sharpton plays politics for Obama', *Politico*, 6 April 2011.

are so heinous they cannot be ignored any more and must be addressed. Allow white people to determine this threshold but come out boldly in support in a bid to 'show leadership'. (*Fox News* may be a good barometer. When *Fox News* accepts that black folk are suffering there must be an outright holocaust.)

7. Take lots and lots and lots of pictures with black people.[5]

8. Appoint some black people to a few subtly black positions (e.g. the diversity department), however, do not even think of hiring more than one black person to key positions in the company. The more the boardroom looks like a Wu-Tang Clan or So Solid album release party, the more the share price suffers.

9. When under pressure to do more for black employees, assertively state that you 'are not the CEO of the black part of the company, but the CEO of the entire company'.

10. Nuclear option: only do this when things are getting really bad and you are in a desperately tough black corner: express support for reparations.

Finally, you must be wary of a vicious and formidable brand of black asshole: the academic and the public intellectual. They are smart, they are committed, they are naturally contrarian, and they are usually right. They are, therefore, somewhat dangerous. Think Cornel West, Yomi Adegoke, Tavis Smiley, Marc Lamont Hill, Sister Souljah, Gary Younge, Kehinde Andrews, Adam Elliott-Cooper, Remi Joseph-Salisbury, Killer Mike and so on. In critical detail below, here is how you deal with such people:

1. Ignore them.

5 'Barack Obama explains why he'll no longer take selfies with people', *Today*, 1 November 2017.

187 Quick Dos and Don'ts: 172–187

172. Do beware of any kind of company-enforced forced jollity, patriotism, activism or diet.

173. Do be prepared to contend with the omnipresent imaginary black friend – the one you never see but always have to argue against. The one who always seems to agree with white people. 'Well, *you* might think that slavery was a very bad thing,' said Raymond 'Ray' Cysm, 'but my black friend thinks it was a great idea and wishes it was brought back.'

174. Do join in with gusto when white supremacist anthems are sung in chorus in a professional setting. 'Sweet Home Alabama', 'Rule Britannia', the theme song of *Friends*, all western national anthems, 'Candle In The Wind' (i.e. the white 'Pour Out A Little Liquor'), etc.

175. Do be willing and ready to instantly forgive any atrocity that you may be subjected to – especially murder.

176. Do note that rhyming words sound more logical and authoritative to the human ear and are therefore a great tool of persuasion. For example, 'beware of the illusion of inclusion and the "farce-sity" of diversity. Especially if you lack the complexion for the protection, promotion and proper compensation.'

177. Do expect the words, names and legacies of your heroes to be used and abused. The strongest weapons in the hands of the oppressor are the minds of the oppressed. The second strongest are the heroes of the oppressed. Especially the dead ones.

178. Do note that white success is collectivised whereas white failure is individualised. The opposite is true for black failure and success.

179. Do pander to white people's need for fairy tales: 'Britain ended slavery', 'the civil war was about the state's rights', 'Brexit is not about race – neither is immigration', 'seasoning is not a necessity' – that sort of thing.

180. Don't ever forget: like money, information and knowledge, white skin is power.

181. Do note the following indicators that it may be time to leave your company:

- Your blood pressure is higher than your credit rating.
- You have happy dreams of pistol-whipping your boss.
- You're dependent on some form of narcotic to get through the day.
- You're spending more than 0.1% of your salary on lottery tickets.
- You subconsciously see the Selma bridge, as opposed to the company logo, when you arrive at work.

182. Do remember that there is no story without struggle. And there is no black experience without white bullshit.

183. Do tick the 'prefer not to say' box in the ethnicity questionnaire when applying for jobs. And if you can find a way to stay in the closet during the interview stage, do so.

184. Don't ever trade your aspirations, your dreams, for any old job.

185. Do start each day with the words of Reginald Lewis: 'Keep going, no matter what.' And then follow it up with what would have been the words of Franklin D. Roosevelt if he'd been black: 'The only thing we have to fear is fear itself. And institutional racism.'

186. Don't forget who you really are, where you came from. And who put you there.

187. Do always remember that at the end of the day there is nothing wrong with you. You are trying to navigate a social order and a stigma that predated you and will continue after you. In a normal and just world, you wouldn't have to go through any of this shit.

CHAPTER 16

Your Power Base and Your Legacy

'This is an impressive crowd. The haves and the have mores.
Some people call you the elite, I call you my base.'

– George W. Bush

Your arc is complete. You've made the transition. You've banked your 'earned' whiteness. And, above all, you've overthrown the White Man.

You've now morphed into what your detractors and/or the hood would call a 'power-crazed happy negro sell-out coon', a 'bitch-ass-nigga' and/or a 'wasteman'. What your mummy and daddy, dependants, subordinates and most of society would call a 'success'.

But you know the truth. You know exactly what you are: you're the last White Man standing. The black Führer. Blührer, if you will.

Screw Theresa May and her swag-free husband, Emmanuel Macron and his former groomer, Steve Bannon and his Tommy Robinson blow-up doll, etc. 'White power' is yours.

The very final hurdle is to make sure white power remains yours for ever. Even after your career is over. Even after you've been welcomed into the hottest corners of hell.

So, you need to secure the one thing that every White Man cherishes just as much as they do power, winning and domination: your legacy. You, like any self-respecting 'great person', want your name and deeds to be remembered for eternity so that your children's children can trade on the jolly fact that they're linked to your reproductive organ (like Sir Nicholas Soames, Winston Churchill's rather talentless though very charming grandson, arguably does).

But hardly any 'powerful' or 'successful' person wants to be remembered for what they really and truly were. Of course not. Everyone wants to be remembered for what they have led people to believe they are. You want people to believe your propaganda and to back it up and treat it as fact. Therefore, you need disciples to be your initial believers and to help spread the 'good news' about your 'amazing work'.

Your propaganda, the good news about your amazing work, is your legacy. And it must be protected at all costs.

The Story of Nelson, Robert and Some White Guy called Winston

Nelson Mandela's legacy is focused around the theme that he was the 'great forgiver', the 'man who propelled South Africa to peace and ended apartheid', which is true and just. The additional unspeakable truth is that, as president, Mandela basically maintained an economic status quo that largely mirrored the one upheld by apartheid.

Robert Mugabe's legacy on the other hand is focused on Zimbabwe's journey from being the breadbasket of Africa to the basket case of Africa'. It's worth remembering that being responsible for the deaths of thousands of Zimbabweans did not stop him becoming Sir Robert Mugabe, 'a knighted good egg' in the eyes of Britain and the West. The additional unspeakable truth is that, as president and rebel leader, he broke the back of white supremacy in his country.

Churchill? Great British war hero but also a blue-blooded white supremacist. Man who stood up to tyranny when tyranny was against him but was simultaneously a tyrant to many others.

To create your legacy, you need back-up. You need a power base, a core constituency who will identify with you, consider you their own, support you through thick and thin, champion you and fight for you when necessary. Perhaps even name some bullshit think tank or charity after you.[1]

Luckily for you, you were born into what will probably be your natural powerbase: black people. So, keeping black people on your side is critical. And it is perhaps the cheapest investment you'll ever make. For when it all goes down – and it eventually will – whether via death, disease, wishing to buy NBC[2] or most probably infidelity-related disgrace – they, black people, will remain your loyal fans. Even your strongest critics will rally to your side. Unless, that is, you do something absolutely beyond the pale, like repeatedly going on *Fox News* and telling black people to pull their pants up or proclaiming 400 years of slavery to have been a 'choice' or becoming a TUT (Tory Uncle Tom).

Black people will build and defend your legacy no matter what – even if it largely worked against their interests. You're a great black person and that is rare. That is precious. You're precious. And therefore, even if your preciousness is based on an orgy of lies, deceit and backstabbing, black people will fight on that lie, and fight for you till the very end.

1 The Mandela Rhodes Foundation: https://mandelarhodes.org.
2 'Conspiracy claims surround Bill Cosby debate', *CNN*, 8 January 2015.

To play it safe, when you're approaching the end of your tenure (assuming white people haven't unexpectedly decapitated you long before then), when you're a lame duck, you might as well use the last few drops of your power to help good old black folk out. Similar to how Barack Obama rediscovered black people in his last months in office (and needed them to vote for his preferred successor).[3] Consider it an insurance premium.

With your legacy sewn up, you have one very final detail to bear in mind. They are the words of the great writer James Baldwin: 'People pay for what they do and still more for what they allow themselves to become. And they pay for it very simply by the lives they lead.'

Now go forth and conquer. Like a White Man.

3 'Obama: it will be "personal insult" if African Americans do not vote', *The Guardian*, 18 September 2016.

Epilogue: Leadership Tips

I n the fantastical event that you have enough corporate and/or global power to restart the clock, and fancy treating yourself by flipping the script on white people, you're unlikely to need further advice, but here are some strategic tips:

Micro Strategies for Monetising White People

Step 1: Funnel as many white people as humanly possible into a particular type of area. Ensure said areas are economically destitute, dangerously too small for the population size, highly polluted, never maintained and void of hope. Give this type of area a somewhat vague yet charming name, perhaps 'The Crap-pits'.

Step 2: Prohibit and criminalise refreshments, treats, recreational substances and merchandise white people love and are accustomed to consuming or making an income out of (e.g. coffee, tea, raisins, quinoa, tobacco, quiche, alcohol, etc).

Step 3: Categorise, brand and demonise the items listed above as 'killer narcotics'.

Step 4: Create a public panic around white people who consume or sell, say, quiche Lorraine. Use every means possible to portray them as the worst people in society – absolute menaces and super predators. Perhaps assign alarmist names to them such as 'quiche baron', 'quiche dealer' and 'quiche-head' (it may not be a bad idea to also stigmatise the newly born offspring of quiche-heads as 'quiche babies').

Step 4.5: Covertly permit a generous supply of killer narcotics (and illicit weapons) into the Crap-pits.

Step 5: Subtly create an all-black working-class police force (peppered with a few token white hires) to proactively, frequently and publicly stop and search white people specifically for these killer narcotics and anything else they can find.

Step 6: Declare an 'All Out War on Killer Narcotics'. Ensure your all-black working-class police force don't wage this 'war' on black people who openly and flagrantly use and possess the 'narcotics' in non-Crap-pit areas. Also turn a blind eye to any violence – up to and including murder – white people may be subject to at the hands of the police.

Step 7: Create black-owned and controlled for-profit prisons to house the white people caught up in the War on Killer Narcotics. Use the prisoners as free labour. Use any counter-culture that may arise from the Killer Narcotics War prison boom as a free source of 'edgy' ideas to be marketed and monetised.

Step 7.5: As the prison population booms chastise and stigmatise white people for 'not raising their children' ... this will help create a pipeline of shamed and economically shut-out people: future prisoners and future profits.

Step 8 (optional): Float the black-owned and white-occupied private prisons on the stock market. Get black Twitter to promote the stock. Sell as it skyrockets and buy-back as it crashes the next day.

Step 9: Find more things that white people do and love that you can criminalise (perhaps afternoon tea, darts or horse racing). And then repeat the first five and a half steps above until you're a multibillionaire, your nation has the largest prison population on earth and white families are decimated en mass for generations.

Final step: bask in your income streams and pray that 'karma' is merely a weird Indian sex manual.

Macro Strategies for Dividing and Conquering White People

1. Promote and empower gingers over brunettes. And then brunettes over gingers. Convince blondes that they're untouchably superior to gingers, brunettes and everyone else.

2. Facilitate the spread of embarrassing rumours about sexual relations in the office, marital breakdowns, erectile dysfunctions, drug habits, etc.

3. During a team meeting, ask everyone to politely and publicly tease everyone else into revealing who they voted for … and their religion.

4. When you become aware of rivalry or hostility between two teams or team leaders, amalgamate them into one team.

5. Create a work dress code based on eye colour. Gently (yet firmly) insist that blue-eyed people wear micro-shorts, green-eyed people wear Bermuda shorts and brown-eyed people wear trousers.

6. Instruct, say, a Scouser to ask a Geordie not to invite a Glaswegian to a company night-out. Quietly tip off some Brummie that Liverpool and Newcastle have teamed up against the Scottish. Find someone who is able to translate the subsequent argument for you.

7. Read up on the following terms: 'British Empire', 'Scramble for Africa' and 'Lyor Cohen/Roc-A-Fella Records' for further ideas.

The world is yours.

APPENDICES

Appendix 1

Risk Assessment:
Types of Black People in the Corporate World

I f we imagine a utopia where politics, discrimination and White Man-ism don't exist and a level playing field does, there are only ever two types of professionals: the workers and the talent. Now, that doesn't mean that workers are not talented, or that talented people are not workers. Workers and talent are just two different categories of employees. In the same way in which there are only ever two outcomes in every game: winning (talent) and losing (workers).

Every firm worth its salt, either implicitly or explicitly, divides all of its employees into these two categories. You're either a worker or you're talent. And it is not hard to tell which one you are.

The workers will work till they drop. Literally. The worker will be paid less, promoted less and will eventually look visibly poorer than the talent.

Talent on the other hand will leap through the ranks. Even when talent shares a corporate grade with a worker, they will be able to afford things workers couldn't fathom. Why? Because they are paid much more for doing the same job. They are paid more because the firm considers them more valuable and harder to replace.

Talent are diamonds. Workers are cubic zirconia. They may look alike but the price tags make the difference as clear as a baby's criminal record.

If you're talent, congratulations, you've made it.

If you're a worker, don't leave in anger, just leave.

To be talent is to have a career. To be a worker is to have either a long- or short-term job.

So how do you become talent? For the black professional especially, this is where the problem kicks in. Becoming talent is not a case of natural selection (nothing is), it is a man-made[1] decision and therefore subject to people's personal prejudices: whether or not people like you or don't like you, whether they relate to you, and how progressive the firm is. Is there an implicit quota (i.e. cap) for senior black staff? And so on.

Performance, of course, plays a part, too, but I reiterate: this book focuses on the *political* aspects of life as a black professional, as it is safe to assume you have been conditioned from birth to work very hard for the man, the White Man ... on the plantation.

Black professionals are divided into talent and workers like any other ethnicity of professionals. But within those divisions there are multiple types of black professionals. Just like there are multiple types of people.

The diversity amongst black people is seldom ever acknowledged, or properly understood. Even we, good ol' kind, meek, gentle and lovely black folk, love to oversimplify the situation. For example, Chris Rock's two types of black people routine (now dropped): Niggas v. Black People.

Given the pressure-cooker environment that black professionals face as a result of being in spaces that are the nurtured habitat of middle-class white people, this lack of understanding

1 It goes without saying that it is likely to be a white man-made decision. And where it really matters, it is likely to be a White Man-made decision, like most important decisions in the world are.

of the diversity amongst black people and black professionals often ends poorly. Usually with underhand accusations of being a turncoat, a sell-out, an Uncle Tom or an Aunt Stacey Dash. An Oreo, Bounty bar or a coconut, if you prefer your deeply bitter derogatory terms to sound a little sweeter. Not that these highly disregarded characters don't exist, but often failing to understand each other can feed the overhasty application of such labels.

So, in order to avoid potential confusion, frustration and disillusion, you need to understand the major different types of black professionals and their motivations, and how other black professionals would fare should one of these blessed souls be associated with them. Joint-enterprise 'charges' are as potent for black people in the corporate world as they are in the street. One black person is all black people.

What follows from here is unique in human history: a qualitative and authoritative 'study' of black people by a black person. Fuck Carl Jung.

The White Person 'Trapped' in Black Skin

Accept it. Just because someone is born with 'black' skin doesn't mean that they have ever lived the black experience. Which is, of course, the very experience that shapes black people.

There are many black people who are black in skin colour only. In the exact same way you can meet a white person who is completely signed up to black culture to such an extent that he or she may well be welcomed with open arms into the Nation of Islam,[2] there are black people so out-there

2 'Farrakhan dines with "my brother" Eminem', USA Today, 4 September 2015.

that they, too, have fully crossed over. We all know them, we all recognise that Alice-in-Wonderland gaze in their eyes, and we all politely suffer the confused and toadying terms they often use to describe themselves and downplay their blackness. Examples include 'Cablinasian', 'Blackglo-Saxons', 'Afri-Aryan Americans' and the patently ludicrous 'European'.

For all intent and purposes, these people are white. Very white. As white as Serena Williams' husband's website. In fact, they're often whiter than most white people (usually the case when you're an outsider trying to compensate for what makes you so).

So how do you identify these peculiar souls with absolute certainty? How do we determine the caucasoïde trapped in a négroïde shell?

By the content of their character of course! The white person who happens to be trapped in black skin is normally quick to unleash romantic catchphrases such as 'there is no race but the human race' and 'I just happen to be black' and 'I don't see colour' and 'of course white people are, on average, great dancers'.

They are likely to deny, or thoroughly downplay, the existence of even obvious racism or any form of discrimination. They are unlikely to have many, or any, black friends or allies. And, when it counts, when it is 'on and popping', fellow black professionals almost naturally feel no need to turn to them for support or input.

But this, too, needs to be clearly understood. Being white while black, i.e. identifying with white people and their cultural and political norms, does not make the white person trapped in black skin a bad person or even a liability. Such a person may be one of the coolest and nicest people in the corporation.

Identifying with a different race is far from problematic (although it may render you less than an asset to fellow black people). Identifying with *racism* (the founding pillar of whiteness) on the other hand does make you a bad person. A very bad person. And sadly, this is not as unusual as you might think.

The 'cool' white-black guy is likely to listen to you when you complain of racism but will do nothing to help. The racist white guy trapped in black skin is likely to charge the person complaining of racism with racism.

In such situations, take comfort in this: though he may see himself as 'different' to other black people, though he may see himself as one and the same as white people, the whitegeist does not and never will. Sooner or later, he, too, will be kicked out of bed.

The Story of Ben Douglas

Ben Douglas is a writer and self-proclaimed 'middle-class black Briton' who owns and runs an international theatre school. By his own admission, he never really lived the black experience and avoided the racism that plagues the lives of other black people, because he was adopted by a middle-class white family as a child (after his mother sadly passed away).

Ben developed a reputation in the British media for being the go-to black guy for opinions white people wanted to hear on issues directly affecting black people. Not dissimilar to Larry Elder[3] or, tragically, Dr Martin Luther King Jr's niece, Alveda King,[4] in America.

3 'Larry Elder: "Uncle Tom" is more destructive than the "N-word"', *Investors Business Daily*, 21 September 2017.
4 'Martin Luther King Jnr.'s pro-life niece reveals on MLK Day she voted for Donald Trump', *Daily Mail*, 16 January 2017.

He didn't really have much time for, or belief in, racism.[5] And all was going well for him until he was stopped by the police while driving his £36,000 car. It was at this moment that the whitegeist snatched the duvet off him.[6] And, boy, did poor little Ben feel the winter's cold.

Highly predictable story cut short: the police firmly reminded him that he was a black man in a white country driving a car that is only expected to be driven by a lighter shade of pale. Which means only one thing: he was a black man in deep trouble.

Though, thankfully, they didn't subject him to a little 'lawful killing', poor little Ben was shaken up to such an extent that he wrote an apology to black people in the same white-wing paper he would previously have gone to complain about black people's 'moaning'.

It becomes progressively easier to deal with the white guy trapped in black skin (both the racist and non-racist editions) when you realise that the best way of dealing with him is to not deal with him. Avoid him. Pray that he either sees the light (i.e. the darkness of whiteness) or that he doesn't reproduce.

5 There are only ever three sorts of people who downplay or dismiss racism: those who haven't lived under the yoke of it, those who have an economic imperative to do so, and racists.
6 'A middle-class black man raised by white parents, Ben had always respected the police. Until one night they stopped his car ...', *Daily Mail*, 15 March 2013.

Key Risk Indicator Matrix[7] for the White Person Trapped in Black Skin

Risk Indicator	Score
Corporate star power (0 to 5)	3
Ruthlessness level (0 to 5)	2
Blackness level (-5 to 0)	0
Revolutionary tendency level (-5 to 0)	-1
White lovability level (0 to 10)	8
General political savvy (0 to 5)	3
Overall potential in the white corporate world score	15
Black-on-black corporate association threat level	Medium

Examples of People Who Give Off White Person Trapped in Black Skin Vibes

1. Tiger Woods, golfing icon who self-identifies as Casblianasian; the police, however, identified him as 'BLACK' (in big black capital letters).

2. Noah Tannenbaum, Meadow Soprano's 'black' boyfriend.

3. Pre-negro wake-up call Ben Douglas, black *Daily Mail* columnist.

7 Where a key risk indicator (KRI) is ranked from zero to five or, in the uniquely potent situation of white lovability, zero to 10 it means that the higher the number the greater success in corporate life the professional will experience. However, where the KRI is ranked from -5 to zero the nearer to zero a professional is the more palatable they are to the white corporate world. For example, a -5 on the blackness scale means you're in Old Dirty Bastard/Kodak Black/post-acquittal OJ Simpson territory: not exactly CEO of Microsoft material. A 9 on white lovability places you in Oprah Winfrey territory. Overall the closer a black professional type is to 25 and further away you are from -10 the better.

4. Pre-Michelle Barack Obama, former President of the United States of America/black Jesus in the flesh.

5. Sinitta Malone, singer and inadvertent white toxic masculinity champion, who confusingly synonymised 'big blue eyes' with being macho.

Johnny Just Come (JJC)

JJC is similar to the white guy trapped in black skin in so far as he doesn't really understand the dynamics of being black in a predominantly white environment. Not because he is lost or confused or 'transracial' but because he just hopped off the boat from Africa.[8] Or the Caribbean. He just touched western soil and drank western Kool-Aid[9] for the first time.

He doesn't understand racism or white privilege or the general bullshit associated with being black. He is full of gusto, full of white saviour movies, completely oblivious to the sharks circling him and joyous in his naïvety.

Also, similar to the white guy trapped in black skin, he doesn't identify with 'black' people. And why would he? Up until this moment he has never been black.

'Never been black?' I hear you ask.

When black people are in Africa they are not black people. They are just people. An African becomes a 'black person' when he disembarks the aeroplane in Europe or America for the first time and the immigration officer looks at his passport. Looks at

8 With apologies to brothers and sisters in white-dominated African nations such as South Africa, Zimbabwe, etc. Especially those who still wear the scars of modernised medieval racism on their backs.

9 As sad irony would have it, western Kool-Aid was actually served in the literal sense in Guyana (the Caribbean). And yes, it was a smiling White Man who served it there too.

him. Looks at his passport again and then looks at him. Sighs from the depths of his heart and let's rip: 'I'll only warn you once. Nigger, keep that big mandingo ding-a-ling out of my precious and pure white blonde daughters. And my unsullied wife. And don't hog all the oxygen with those big ugly nostrils. Welcome to America, nigger.'

A Nigerian in Nigeria is not a black person. He is just a person. And is therefore unlikely to be equipped to deal with all the baggage associated with being black over a protracted period because he has never had to. It doesn't mean that he hasn't faced difficulty; far from it. It just means that he hasn't faced this particularly vicious brand of difficulty.

JJC may be able to tell you stories of being chained to a table and having his nipples electrocuted for a parking violation, but he cannot tell you anything about, say, race-based structural discrimination. In the same way, the average black person in Europe or America would struggle to tell him about what a structural adjustment programme is, how it works in practice and how it kills.

Similar to the white guy trapped in black skin, he, too, will annoyingly question the need for empowerment initiatives such as a black professionals' network ('But white people don't have one'), he will tell you that you complain of racism too much ('You don't know how good you have it, back home for the cost of this burger we could feed and educate an entire village for three months and you complain about racism? Shut up your mouth, foolish boy'). And so on and so forth.

But don't write him off just yet, as he may still prove useful and powerful.

A camel will waltz through a needle's eye before an unconnected random black person will land on western shores and attain a heavily sought-after role. It doesn't matter how qualified you are, you have to mop the floor, drive a cab, sell a kidney, etc. for a few decades and perhaps then your children or grandchildren will be given a shot. Who the hell do you think you are? A Boer or an Aussie?[10]

A black person who has just arrived in a western country and found himself in a choice professional role quickly is likely to be from a privileged background. He is probably the child or highly favoured relative of a diplomat, successful business person or powerful politician in Pipelineria.

Either that or he just graduated from an Ivy League college ... which means, once again, that he is probably the child or highly favoured relative of a diplomat, successful business person or powerful politician in Pipelineria.

Once JJC has been wholesomely welcomed to Whypipoland and stung numb, he will completely identify with the usual black experience and therefore black people. This is likely to result in one of two things: he will either pack his bags and quietly return to where he came from (meaning he'll go from JJC to IJGB, I Just Got Back), or he will stand up for himself.

If he does the latter, he could prove quite useful and, depending on the extent of the importance of his connections in the old country, he could prove to be a formidable challenger to the white power structure. And therefore, a new-found asset of fellow black professionals.

What are his prospects? Similar to the white guy trapped in black skin, JJC will be viewed in a favourable light in a professional setting (once the powers that be get over his accent). He is likely to be considered refreshing and lovely. Provided he is a good performer and works harder than his white peers, he may be given a shot. He could go far. Especially if the company is dependent on his connections back home in Pipelineria.

10 I'm certain my Indigenous Australian brothers and sisters understand that when people say 'Aussie' in the West they're not the image that immediately springs to mind.

Key Risk Indicator Matrix for Johnny Just Come

Risk Indicator	Score
Corporate star power (0 to 5)	3.5
Ruthlessness level (0 to 5)	2
Blackness level (-5 to 0)	-1
Revolutionary tendency level (-5 to 0)	-2
White lovability level (0 to 10)	8
General political savvy (0 to 5)	2.5
Overall potential in the white corporate world score	13
Black-on-black corporate association threat level	Low

Examples of People Who Give Off JJC Vibes

1. Chimamanda Ngozi Adichie, never knowingly underquoted Nigerian writer who landed in America and rejected the notion of an African–American calling her 'sister'. Nowadays she won't think twice before calling out white supremacy by its name.

2. Fela Kuti, upper middle-class Nigerian child radicalised into ultra-afrocentric black militancy after tasting British and American racism for the first time.

3. Lupita Nyong'o, Queen of Katwe and kickass of Wakanda.

4. Sir Trevor McDonald OBE, Trinidadian-born journalist who rose to become the face of Britain's main news bulletins, and, pre Rastamouse, the most trusted and beloved black man in Britain.

5. Tidjane Thiam, enigmatic French-Ivorian banking executive, CEO of Credit Suisse.

The Story of Tina, the Streets in a Suit

It's Monday morning, you're armed with an expensive coffee (which you don't even like the taste of) and waiting for the lift in a crowded lobby. The lift arrives, and of course you let everyone on before you as, hey, they're white and you don't want them to think you're some impolite, inconsiderate, violent black savage who is about to rob and kill them. And then make sweet and sweaty interracial love to their corpses.

The lift is packed and the door is closing. You take a swig of your skinny latte with an espresso shot (decaf) in a bid to demonstrate your sophistication and you smile at everyone who makes eye contact in order to prove that you're a 'good one'. And that you're not going to relieve the blonde lady of her tightly clutched handbag. Or purity.

As the lift's doors are about to shut, a foot encased in brand spanking new sand-coloured Timberlands slams into view, forcing them to re-open. Then you're slapped round the face by the sound of some DMX album blazing through headphones. You look up and see a single gold front tooth glinting from a beaming smile – she caught the lift.

Half Blood, half Crip and as gangsta as Putin's Russia, it's Tina, the streets in a suit.

Sporting her trademark durag to cover her jail cornrows, an oversized Avirex jacket covers her suit and tie. Top-of-the-range Beats by Dre cover her ears. Hysterics, fear and 'What These Bitches Want' engulfs the lift.

You close your eyes and offer up a quick prayer: 'Dear Lord, you put me here with these white people, please don't let Tina see me and erode FOUR YEARS of hard work, good whitewill and ...'

'What it do, cuz?! What was the weekend saying?'

Fuck. You open your eyes and the very worst has happened.

Tina's fist is pointed in your direction waiting for yours to return what Fox News *would call a 'terrorist fist jab'.[11] Against every instinct in your body, you oblige. Your fist meets hers. Sweat meets the crease of your bottom and gently glides down to form a small lake in your crotch area.*

Before you can respond, she continues, becoming progressively more animated: 'Was up in Magic City on Saturday. Them females was going in, son, yanadamean, YANADAMEAN!!' She fist jabs you again.

Your blackest nightmare has now fully materialised. Nonetheless you recite yet another calm prayer in your head: 'HELP! HELP! GOD HELP! DO SOMETHING! SWING DOWN, SWEET CHARIOT ...'

Your god lets you down again. Tina keeps going.

'You hear what happened though? Sharon's baby daddy and his other baby mama got shot by MC Toe Tag's crew outside the club. Flesh wounds though – in and out – nothing too serious.'

Suddenly she stops. She feels the white gaze on her. She looks back, cuts her eyes at them, kisses her teeth and returns to the conversation. 'His people's knife game was on fleek tho. They handled business. Immediate justice.'

Then, thankfully, she arrives at her floor and gets off. But not before she can hammer the final nail into your coffin. 'You owe me lunch, brother. Don't leave me hanging!' says Tina.

You respond with the only word you have so far contributed the entire lift ride: 'Absolutely.'

'My nigga,' she responds as she diddy-bops away, affectionately throwing up a gang sign.

11 'Fox news anchor taken off air after Obama "terrorist fist jab" gaffe', *The Guardian*, 13 June 2008.

The streets in a suit is often a lovely person. Refreshingly frank and completely honest in how he carries himself, how he speaks and the fact that he doesn't give a damn about progressing within the organisation or how he is perceived, he keeps it 100% real.

He is going nowhere.

He is not a bad guy. However, he is a complete liability for the ambitious black professional.

His 'uncompromising' demeanour has rendered him a spectacle for white people in the office and any other black person who stands too close to him may absorb some of his brand. And lack of prospects. As they say, 'Show me your friend and I'll show you who you are.'

Show me your friend and I'll show you your future bank statement.

As a result of this, sadly, the ambitious, going-places black professional will have to avoid the streets in a suit. Especially when other (white) colleagues are around. His brand is naturally toxic. And he will drag you down.

What makes all of this particularly unfortunate is that the streets in a suit naturally understands the issues facing the black professional. So, he should be a valuable asset, but his approach, which is essentially a lack of approach, renders him all but useless to collective progression.

The fact that he knows and understands the issues at stake may be one reason why he has decided to completely shun the entire game.

Sometimes spectating is more rewarding than playing. It certainly is when you've got a rap career and multiple other side hustles to focus on. Which, believe it or not, may mean that the streets in a suit has the last laugh.

Key Risk Indicator Matrix for the Streets in a Suit

Risk Indicator	Score
Corporate star power (0 to 5)	0
Ruthlessness level (0 to 5)	1
Blackness level (-5 to 0)	-5
Revolutionary tendency level (-5 to 0)	-3
White lovability level (0 to 10)	1
General political savvy (0 to 5)	0
Overall potential in the white corporate world score	-6
Black-on-black corporate association threat level	Extremely High

Examples of People Who Give Off Streets in a Suit Vibes

1. Suge Knight, American footballer turned gang member turned bodyguard turned genius/ruthless record executive turned gang member turned prisoner. Red suit aficionado.

2. Rasheeda (from *Insecure*), the summer intern at Molly Carter's law firm – lovely, smart and uber 'authentic' young lady who blew her summer internship ... for being a little too 'authentic' for the white powers that be in her firm.

3. 99.9% of all black people under the age of forty who work in the post room or on the IT Help Desk. For example, Bony T in *Boomerang*.

4. Thugnificent (*The Boondocks*), rapper turned UPS delivery driver.

5. Every single SoundCloud-level rapper who holds down a nine-to-five office job while pursuing their dreams.

The Undercover Brother

From the top, the undercover brother is not to be trifled with.

You can see it in his eyes, hear it in his tone (if your black-dar is fine-tuned enough you can spot a black person by the bass in their tone alone), feel it in his soul and swagger. He is 100% a black person in black skin. He is not a street guy, rap star, dough boy or road man. And, unlike Johnny Just Come, he isn't essentially a tourist with a good job. He is a brother, or he should be, but he is 'undercover'; he is hiding, pretending and conniving. He is an undercover brother (or sister, but as the patriarchy still has a little breath in it we'll settle for brother).

Well adjusted, well educated, oozing social as well as cultural capital, competence and excellence, he is classic black professional class.

And therefore, he gets it. He knows what is going on. He understands the complications that being black add to his career prospects. Yet, perhaps in order to cope with it or overcome it, he accommodates all of the race-related shenanigans that the corporate world chucks in his direction. And, perhaps unknowingly, he now identifies with it (or he eventually will).

The key thing to remember with regard to the undercover brother is that it's a coping mechanism. He is deep cover because that is what he feels he has to do to get by and get up.

The undercover brother should be spearheading the solution.

In fact, he should be the solution. But he is not. Yet, as tempting as it is to simply dismiss him as part of the problem, it would be unfair to do so without context.

The problem existed long before the undercover brother did and will exist long after he joins his ancestors or strengthens the firm's alumni.

The problem as he sees it is this: he is a natural outsider desperate to become an insider. He is a black person swimming firmly against the tide in an implicitly segregated *Nie Blankes* ocean.

He wants to get to the top, he understands what it takes, and therefore he knows that he has what it takes. Part of his plan for getting to the top is to make the dominant components of his environment – for clarity, white people – as comfortable and happy as possible. And that means dominant components from the top right the way to the bottom.

This desire to please, to assimilate (in order to accumulate) and to create a comfortable environment in order to be appreciated and elevated can be quite dangerous when taken to the extreme, particularly for other black professionals.

Example: every black professional who has been a professional for a reasonable period of time has suffered some form of humiliation in professional life. Sometimes these belittling acts are deliberate, sometimes they are not. The key thing is that they are belittling and as a result sometimes serve as a source of entertainment or titillation to (white) colleagues.

The undercover brother will not let such moments pass him by when they happen to a black professional in his presence. No way. Not ever. He will seize the opportunity to ingratiate himself with the good white folk of the company by further amplifying your embarrassment and reducing you to a joke. Even on sacred stuff. Your braid fell out? He'll pick it up, run behind you and hand it to you, turn to the nearest white chick and say, 'Never had to do that for you, Becky ... wonder why?' Enjoying a soul-comforting plate of last night's jollof for lunch, undercover brother will let rip, 'I can't stand the smell of that peasant food. Can't you go and eat it in the loo? Yuck. Give me risotto any day.'

He may even ask questions he knows you won't be able to answer and then ask a member of staff subordinate to you to answer the question.

He needs to be loved and he acts in a manner that suggests that the only way white people will love him is if black people loathe him. Or at least consider him to be foreign to them.

God forbid you're ever subject to some degree of overt racism in the presence of the undercover brother. Because you'll be bitterly disappointed. His ambition-driven eagerness to please may make him side with the perpetrator, i.e. white people.

The Story of Kwasi

Eton, Cambridge and Harvard-educated Kwasi Kwarteng is Britain's brightest and most ambitious politician. Kwasi is also a classic undercover brother.

In order to get to where he is and where he is going to, Kwasi has made a lot of dangerous compromises. He compromised on:

- *His relationship with any respectable black barber (hence his hairline is as fucked up as a colonial map's border);*
- *His relationship with any other black MPs;*[12]

12 'There's one black Tory MP in particular. I won't mention his name. OK, Kwasi … really doesn't like talking to black people in case somebody realises he is black.' – Dawn Butler MP see 'Labour's Dawn Butler sparks second furore with claims black Tory MP "prefers white people"', *Brent and Kilburn Times*, 18 January 2016.

- *His plate of Basmati jollof at any communal parties after he joined a band of merry anti-immigrant bigots to compromise the nation's relationship with its biggest trading partner;*
- *The reputation of his optician and the integrity of his love life by falling for former Home Secretary Amber Rudd (never to be mistaken for Amber Rose);*
- *His relationship with Britain's black community.*

It is on the last two, related compromises that he went too far.

In early 2018, it emerged that the Home Office (then led by the aforementioned Amber Rudd) had been deporting black citizens (mainly of Jamaican origin) 'in error'. This left unknown scores of black people in debt, despair, destitution and/or death.

Naturally, the ruling Conservative Party needed some chocolate to go out to the world and proclaim that their clearly racist policies which led to these deportations (and deaths) were not racist after all. They turned to our brother, their undercover brother, Kwasi Kwarteng.

Sweaty and at times incoherent, he got the job done. In the process, he solidified his status and future in the Conservative Party and infamy in the black community.

The undercover brother has decided to align himself with – i.e. prostrate himself before – people (white people) who can help him get somewhere. Strictly business, strictly strategy.

Where black folk are useful to the undercover brother is as props to demonstrate that he is 'different'. That he is unique, that he is the one in 10,000 (as Calvin Candie would have put it), part of the talented tenth (as W.E.B. Du Bois would have put it), the exceptional and extraordinary new black (as Pharrell Williams would have put it).

The undercover brother will do everything to defend and justify sometimes unspeakable actions by the corporation. He is the firm's go-to chocolate who will be pushed forward to attest to how progressive and forward-leaning the business is when the questions start coming. He will swear that the firm is an 'equal opportunity' employer and restate the world-renowned patent lie that 'if you're good enough you should apply, you'll get the job and excel'. He'll probably publicly oppose playing field-levelling initiatives such as affirmative action for the firm. He will happily be the lipstick on the firm's *Potemkin village* diversity scheme pig.

The power structure will eventually consider him someone they can do business with. He could one day form a critical part of the business, in the same way that Stephen was critical to the operations of the Candyland plantation in *Django Unchained*. Like Stephen and the lady who sang the final verse on Dr Dre's classic ode to gallantry 'Bitches Ain't Shit', he is a classic compassion-free collaborator.

So how far could he go?

The prospects for the undercover brother are quite bright. He is a shrewd and savvy operator. He doesn't care who he steps on to get to where he needs to be. He especially doesn't care if a few fellow black professionals are crushed under the wheels of his bus. He will not allow himself to be ghettoised and he doesn't suffer from any form of emotional baggage. Above all: he is the exact sort of person who will read this book and swear by every single squalid suggestion made in it.

Bastards like this go far. Very far.

Key Risk Indicator Matrix for the Undercover Brother	
Risk Indicator	Score
Corporate star power (0 to 5)	4.5
Ruthlessness level (0 to 5)	5
Blackness level (-5 to 0)	-0.5
Revolutionary tendency level (-5 to 0)	0
White lovability level (0 to 10)	10
General political savvy (0 to 5)	5
Overall potential in the white corporate world score	24
Black-on-black corporate association threat level	Extremely High

Examples of People Who Give Off Undercover Brother Vibes

1. Eunice Rivers Laurie, the African American nurse who, from 1932 to 1972, coordinated the horrendously unethical 'Study of Untreated Syphilis in the Negro Male' (popularly known as the Tuskegee syphilis experiment). The 'participants' were never informed that they had syphilis and were never administered drugs known to cure syphilis.

2. Lightfoot Solomon Michaux, televangelist who collaborated with J. Edgar Hoover's FBI to discredit Dr Martin Luther King.

3. Omarosa Manigault-Newman, reality TV uber-villain, staunch Trump loyalist, black pariah in absolute terms turned conqueror of the Trump machine. Arguably an undercover brother as well as the 'spook' who sat by the door, given that she clearly infiltrated the Trump regime.

4. Sheriff David Clarke, horror movie-worthy black cop, Democrat and a white supremacist's wet dream come true.

5. Trevor Phillips OBE, former Chair of the Equality and Human Rights Commission. Went from being a young man whose foot was never far from a racist's bottom to being an old man whose lips are never far from a racist's bottom.

The Office Revolutionary

The Story of Shanice

The time is 9 a.m., hump day, and Dr Mildred Dylan, an external management training consultant[13] is in the office to provide an all-day training session titled 'Prioritising: Effectively Managing Time and Expectations'.

Mildred welcomes everyone and then starts the utterly predictable exchange of names and the tell-a-funny-story-about-yourself routine. Once that pain has subsided and everyone's fake smile muscles are relaxed, she launches into the meat and greens of the session.

---

13 Slick, waffling hustler on £1,600 a day, who is almost certainly a friend of one of the company's big white cheeses.

'Right, let's get down to the fun bit,' she says, in full game-show-host mode. 'Efficiency is critical. Efficiently managing your time means that you can efficiently manage expectations. Efficiently managing expectations means that you efficiently manage your career. Do you see where this is going?'

Sensing boredom from her suicide-inducing management speak, she pauses, and then decides that some interactivity may work well to engage the class at this point. 'Who has heard of the concept known as the Pareto Principle?' Mildred asks, glancing encouragingly around the room.

A well-manicured, shea-buttered, milk chocolate hand with red, black and green beads on the associated wrist is launched firmly and calmly into the air.

'Brilliant!' says Mildred. 'Thank you, Shanice! Would you like to explain the Pareto Principle as a concept to our gathering of friends?'

Shanice rises to her feet.

'No need to stand up. It's a relaxed environment here,' says Mildred.

'I'd rather stand, thank you … The Pareto Principle is a concept that suggests that, for many events and achievements, 80% of the results or effects come from 20% of the causes. An example would be if 80% of our sales came from 20% of our clients. It implies, perhaps implicitly, that not everyone is of equal importance and significance.'

'Thank you so much, Shan—'

'Excuse me. The Pareto Principle was named after the Italian economist, political scientist and philosopher Vilfredo Pareto,' interrupts Shanice, before pausing for effect.

'But who was Vilfredo Pareto?' Mildred steps back and arranges her features into that very white middle-class expression that suggests she is genuinely interested in what Shanice has to say next.

'Who was this wretched man? Vilfredo Pareto was the father of fascism in Italy. His ideology, which I just laid out for you, was the very basis on which Mussolini-led Italian fascism rose to power,' she says, reinforcing each point with a fist slammed on the table.

The room is stunned into silence. Mildred's cleavage, neck and face are turning increasingly bright pink, in either embarrassment or fear. She looks as if she may explode at any given second.

Calmly, Shanice keeps going. 'I'm sorry, Dr Dylan, but this, too, must be said. It is extremely insensitive and against all concepts of being an ally to our Jewish brothers and sisters and many others — but mainly them — to provoke their pain and memory of everything that happened during the war by bringing up this wretched man. As I mentioned, Pareto was the father of Italian fascism. No one would dare teach a class on management or efficiency and start it by bringing up, say, something called "Hitler's Principle". Even though I hear Hitler did some admirable work to promote the vegan movement. If you won't bring up Hitler, don't bring up Pareto. Pareto and Hitler? Two cheeks of the same imperialist, racist, white supremacist, misogynist, hairy backside.'

Shanice sits down. No one knows where to look.

Flushed, sweaty and crimson-faced, Mildred attempts to salvage some degree of normality. 'Erm ... thanks for that, Shanice ... well, who fancies a quick break? It's nine twenty now, shall we reconvene, at say, half ten?'

Shanice is the hard-left (or right, but 1,001 times out of 1,000, left) activist, the social-justice warrior who has stumbled into corporate life. The black revolutionary ... in the office ... And thus the office revolutionary.

The office revolutionary is driven by a desire to make the world, but initially the company, a better and more egalitarian place. She believes a new world is possible and she is acting on those beliefs. She cares little for the profit motive and attains greater career satisfaction by helping people and grandstanding.

The heart of the office revolutionary is assuredly in the right place. And for the most part you have to admire her. She is brave, bold and brash. She doesn't suffer fools. And she doesn't have time for the politics of compromise or compassion. In fact, she doesn't have time for politics, period. She is a classic populist. In a corporate environment.

The office revolutionary is more likely to be armed with statistics about inequality, infant mortality or black youth unemployment than she is figures that are directly pertinent to the growth of the business.

Of course, she is going nowhere. Other than, eventually, through the front door or the window. Probably with a cardboard box that matches her lovely brown complexion.

Perhaps better than any other type (i.e. stereotype) of black professional, the office revolutionary understands the issues at hand. She 100% gets it. She knows exactly what is stacked against her. She understands pretty much every form of -ism that will be thrown at her or will stand in her way. And she is prepared – with the right rhetoric – to deal with them.

And therein lies part of the problem. She is prepared with the right rhetoric to deal with the ills of inequality, racism and risotto, but she is not prepared politically to deal with them. If she was, she would realise that her willingness to speak up and employ her rhetorical skill in situations that require her to be politically savvy and say nothing, or just say less, is bad politics.

Like any self-respecting revolutionary, the office revolutionary will feel the need to hold power to account. Or to attempt to topple power. Or, at the very least, to expose power for the hypocrites and corrupt pigs she considers them to be (and usually are).

'*Fortes fortuna juvat*!' she tells herself. Sadly, it doesn't. The brave get beheaded. Rewatch *Braveheart* if you don't believe me.

At her core, the office revolutionary is a good person. Wanting a better world is a good thing. Trying to expose wrongdoing is a good thing. But as far as businesses are concerned, making money is better than a good thing. It is even better than the best thing. It's the only thing.

The office revolutionary may be great at her job, she may even be the best at it, but it won't make an iota of difference. Even when she is demonstrating legitimate concern about something to do with the business, either her soiled reputation or terrible timing for asking questions will raise questions about her suitability.

When it boils down to it, the office revolutionary represents significant risk. She is a potential whistle-blower, a litigation risk, a reputational risk and therefore a major business and operational continuity risk. If she is left to her own devices, she could destroy the business. Something she'd probably find quite satisfying.

She represents a clear career risk for her fellow black professionals. Particularly the ambitious ones.

The willingness of the career-minded black professional to compromise, to play the game and to be political will infuriate and alienate the office revolutionary. Her worldview is 'liberty or death', the ambitious black professional's is 'money and power or debt and death'.

Even though she'd make a great and steadfast ally, it's best to steer clear of the office revolutionary – when in view of white colleagues at least.

As admirable as she may be, as good at her job as she may be, there is no room for the office revolutionary in corporate life. Sooner or later, one way or another, she'll be shown the door. Or she'll find it herself.

And you'll know when that day arrives, as she'll be outside with a megaphone waging warfare against the man. The White Man. *Viva la office revolución!*

Key Risk Indicator Matrix for the Office Revolutionary	
Risk Indicator	Score
Corporate star power (0 to 5)	1
Ruthlessness level (0 to 5)	1.5
Blackness level (-5 to 0)	-5
Revolutionary tendency level (-5 to 0)	-5
White lovability level (0 to 10)	0
General political savvy (0 to 5)	1
Overall potential in the white corporate world score	-6.5
Black-on-black corporate association threat level	Extremely High

People Who Give Off Office Revolutionary Vibes

1. Pretty much any black union representative.

2. Claudia Jones, Trinidadian journalist, activist, black nationalist, feminist and communist. Moved to America as a child, was deported for political reasons and then moved to Britain where she established Britain's first black paper, *West Indian Gazette*.

3. Cousin Angie (Angela Rye), badass CNN contributor, known for making mincemeat of white men daily.

4. Reverend Jeremiah Wright, Barack Obama's 'spiritual adviser' and America's G-checker.

5. Munroe Bergdorf, model, activist and teller of uncomfortable truths. Fired from a L'Oréal – sigh – diversity campaign for stating that white people are the 'most violent and oppressive force of nature on Earth'. It may have been mentioned somewhere that she is a 'teller of uncomfortable truths'?

The Shook One

The Story of Phil

The first shook one I ever noticed was a guy called Phil, a fifty-something bespectacled brother with a remarkably unkept hairline. (Poor finishing on a hair style is a dead giveaway for a shook one.) I met him at an away-day drinks thing.

We spoke for a few minutes, and throughout he seemed somewhat uncomfortable. So, I felt the need to say something so thunderously black that it would definitely help him to relax a little. 'Don't you just hate butternut squash soup?' And just like that, within minutes, he was speaking freely and happily. He was at ease. Throughout our ten-minute chat I always spoke from the perspective of a person welcoming him to the business.

With his breath smelling like day three of a three-day chemsex orgy, James, a twenty-something empty lard barrel/'I never went to university and look how far I've got' type was walking in our direction. I immediately dragged him into the conversation with Phil and me. Phil's demeanour reverted to type. Thinking little of it, I introduced them.

'Phil? You're introducing me to Phil? He's been here for fifteen years! I should introduce him to you. He's my star employee, aren't you, Phil?' said James.

Phil responded with an uncomfortable smile.

Abruptly cutting a long story short, within fifteen minutes of my inviting him into our conversation, James publicly coerced Phil to hop on stage and perform a karaoke rendition of Coolio's 'Gangsta's Paradise' for the gathering. Lord knows where the karaoke machine came from.

After initially pushing back several times, Phil reluctantly accepted. As he began his attempt to rap, it quickly became clear that he was no Rakim.

Watching Phil's woefully poor, forced rendition of Coolio's classic was like watching a lion at the circus. You could see it in Phil's eyes, in the same way you can see it in a lion's eyes: he didn't want to be there and he certainly didn't want to perform this demeaning garbage.

Take away the social order and the environment that makes it safe for the ringmaster and, of course, the lion would have him for lunch. But you can't take it away. The lion remains at the mercy of the ringmaster. As far as Phil was concerned, James was a great ringmaster. A real P.T. Barnum, Vince McMahon or Alastair Campbell.

He began to sweat profusely and was obviously embarrassed to death but he kept going. By the time he ended, James asked everyone to 'give it up for MC Philly!'. Phil got a roar of applause from the drunken (largely white) crowd. His shirt was soaking wet, and moments later I noticed him quietly leave. That night, I nearly cried myself to sleep for the poor guy.

One of the most heart-breaking sights to behold in professionalism, from a black perspective, is the shook one.

Far from a killer, and even further from a hundred-dollar biller, the shook one is the black professional who has been broken by corporate life. Most likely broken by being black in corporate life.

Completely worn down to the point that she is neither heard or seen. And scared absolutely stiff. Scared to the point of total irrelevance. To the point that opening her mouth to voice an opinion is a shockingly rare occasion. When she does pipe up, it may be preceded or concluded with some form of apology or deprecatory gesture.

'I'm so sorry but can I please suggest … That's my suggestion … I hope I didn't upset anyone … If I did, please accept my profuse apologies …'

It's not surprising that she usually flies under the radar. Silent and easy not to notice. But her silence, sadly, is not some grandiose power-grab strategy or the creep of a leopard, it is fear in manifestation.

Beyond a good performer, she is great. The shook one will be one of the hardest-working professionals you'll ever meet. She is like Boxer in *Animal Farm* or Beatrice and Eugenie in the royal family. She will do all the heavy lifting. And not complain. She will just keep on doing the hard work. And sadly, like Boxer, she will probably end up dog meat (or, against all odds, working a normal day job and only known for wearing silly hats) when all is said and done.

Regardless of how unreasonable or unfair, no matter what is asked of her, she'll get on with it. She'll just do it. Even if that means staying in the office literally overnight or for multiple days. The fear of facing the wrath or provoking the irritation of pretty much anyone is too much for her to bear.

Meek to a fault, one can only hope she inherits the Earth for she stands to gain nothing in the corporation. She will have the career highs of a doormat and the career prospects of the most luxurious sheet of toilet tissue.

She'll be severely and noticeably underpromoted and underpaid but she'll stay put nonetheless. Perhaps she fears change, perhaps she just fears the unknown, or perhaps she has just become a creature of comfort. Or maybe the White Man broke her in a previous role and this has rendered her absolutely petrified of reliving such a traumatic experience. So, she stays put and puts up with whatever is thrown at her.

She will not rock the boat for anything.

As is often the case at circuses, one day the lion will snap and take action to right the wrongs against it. The shook one will eventually reach that point. One day, enough will be enough. And she will eventually stand up for herself.

Until then it's ass up, face down. Like Phil, she will continue to live a life that is, in some regards, as demeaning as life would have been for a black commoner in the West as many as eighty years ago. People will take liberties, because they can. Because she lets them. And she lets them because she is scared and broken.

The shook one poses a near-zero risk to fellow black professionals. A sheep in sheep's clothing, she is completely passive and extremely unlikely to present any career contagion factors. Because she nearly doesn't exist.

Even when she is present she is absent.

Key Risk Indicator Matrix for the Shook One	
Risk Indicator	Score
Corporate star power (0 to 5)	0.75
Ruthlessness level (0 to 5)	0.25
Blackness level (-5 to 0)	-2
Revolutionary tendency level (-5 to 0)	-0.0025
White lovability level (0 to 10)	1
General political savvy (0 to 5)	0.25
Overall potential in the white corporate world score	0.2475
Black-on-black corporate association threat level	Neutral

Examples of People Who Give Off Shook One Vibes

1. Scooby Doo and Shaggy, the legendarily shook duo. Shaggy is off-white but his loyalty to bitch-ass Scooby makes him an honorary brother.

2. David Lammy (2000–2015 era), widely derided bespectacled British politician who, in 2015, finally lost his glasses, lost some weight, found his roar and found black people. Has since made the transition from Kylie to Killmonger … from Bagger Vance to Bernie Grant.

3. Tisean 'T.T.' Williams, distraught single mother whose only child was removed from her custody as she could not afford to care for her. Joined an all-female gang. Unjustly murdered by a white cop during a bank robbery.

> **4.** John Coffey (*The Green Mile*), falsely imprisoned, eight-foot black man complete with superpowers to cure white people of all sorts. Can't seem to save himself from execution.
>
> **5.** Kelly Wright, *Fox News* host whom the company tried to make the 'corporate Jim Crow'.[14]

White Chocolate

Might you have a friend, a ride-or-die homie, who happens to be white? Of course you do! According to the Public Religion Research Institute you have at least eight white friends.[15] Whereas your black ass, on the other hand, is probably the only negro in your white friend's phone book.

The implicit, pertinent point embedded into the above question is this: is there a white person in your 'crew', your damn near all-black inner circle bar eight (you reverse racist, you) who is white but, you know, kind of doesn't feel 'white'?

She is kind of like white chocolate. Put on a blindfold and she feels like chocolate, smells like chocolate, tastes like chocolate ... but take off the blindfold and, to human amazement, she is chocolate but ... white. White chocolate.

The white-person-trapped-in-black-skin phenomenon also works in reverse (kind of like many intellectually bankrupt, racist white people reading this book would like to think racism does): there are black people trapped in white skin. As a type of black professional, we refer to them as 'white chocolate'.

As a type of 'black professional', you say? No, it is not

14 'New Lawsuit Alleges Reporter Kelly Wright Viewed as "Jim Crow" of *Fox News*', *Law and Crime*, 26 April 2017.
15 'Three quarters of whites don't have any non-white friends', *The Washington Post*, 27 November 2014.

a typo. You read correctly. White chocolate has as much a *right* to be considered a black professional as the 'white guy trapped in black skin' does. She gets the culture, the experience, and feels part of it. And wants it to be known that she is part of it.

Hence white chocolate is perhaps the most intriguing type of black professional, for, of course, she is not really black. Biologically, certainly not – none of us are! – but culturally, socially and politically? She is blacker than the back of your neck.

White chocolate idolises black people, black culture and black cultural icons, and she knows a thing or two about black history. Perhaps she even played with black dolls. Therefore, she feels 100% 'at home' in the midst of black people. And most black people feel exactly the same about her.

She understands all of the niche references and wisecracks, and laughs at intra-subtle (and ultra-subtle) black jokes without being prompted (or requiring a thoroughly detailed, joy-crushing explanation) or causing offence. From 'Brown Skin Lady' to 'Back That Ass Up' and right the way down to 'Half On A Baby', she is culturally astute and in sync.

White chocolate oozes soul, coolness and consciousness – and many other 70s blaxploitation movie stereotypes too. Even how she talks – her diction, the bass in her tone and her choice of words – suggests that she has been possessed with some form of black Holy Ghost. She puts the 'negro' in old negro spiritual.

Politically? Ever been an outsider trying to get in? (If your answer to that question is no, then I thank you for needlessly spending your hard-earned money on this book.) The outsider always has to find a way (and possibly ways) to compensate, to go that bit further, to get over whatever has rendered her an outsider.

In black professional circles, white chocolate makes up for

what renders her an outsider – her lack of melanin – by being razor-sharp on black political issues, in an honest and legitimate manner.

As a result, white allies don't get better than white chocolate. She will throw it down in a heartbeat when she sees wrong-doing towards a black person. Well, one she is familiar with at least. She will probably tip off 'fellow' black professionals about something happening to them or said behind their backs: she's a pseudo Robin Hood figure taking from the racist and giving to the black. Our own double agent.

She will understand white privilege, white supremacy and all other forms of crazed white criminality; she will understand racism, systematic discrimination and other plights facing black people. She has either made the effort to study it or she has just absorbed an understanding of it from her surroundings – both black and white.

Many would dismiss or mistake white chocolate for a 'wigger'. It is an easy error or insult to make as the overlap is clear between white chocolate and a wigger. They have both absorbed and adopted black culture.

The difference is that the wigger is not really attracted to black culture, politics and the social experience. Or even black people. He is attracted only to the more troubling corners of black youth culture. Notably the more vulgar, exciting, often pointlessly rebellious, unintentionally homoerotic[16] and self-debasing aspects of low-income black youth culture.

White chocolate, however, is not someone who fell in love with Dr Dre's *The Chronic* album as a prepubescent teen and figured that she wanted to live out the real-life version of the 'Let Me Ride' video. This is not a phase. She is someone who really feels part and parcel of the community, the culture and

16 See many a DMX video for an example of this.

the camaraderie. Her soul is truly black. She automatically feels part of the family. And as such she almost certainly hates Elvis, Vanilla Ice and, more recently, Iggy Azalea. And that, my friends, is the mark of true blackness.

Blacker than Eazy-E's business practices, Jehri Curl and family structure she may be, but what are the prospects for white chocolate in the corporate white world?

She's white! White chocolate may have the soul of a slave but she still has the skin of a slavemaster. And in our white-dominated world that is priceless. Downside-less. So, unless she feels the need to do something daft, like growing dreadlocks, burning incense in the boardroom, or insisting the team night out be a Kevin Hart movie, then she can go as far as any other white person.

Whiteness works in mysterious ways ... even when it is black on the inside.[17]

Key Risk Indicator Matrix for White Chocolate	
Risk Indicator	Score
Corporate star power (0 to 5)	4
Ruthlessness level (0 to 5)	3
Blackness level (-5 to 0)	0
Revolutionary tendency level (-5 to 0)	-2.5
White lovability level (0 to 10)	10
General political savvy (0 to 5)	4
Overall potential in the white corporate world score	18.5
Black-on-black corporate association threat level	N/A[20]

17 'Word to your mother!' as Marky Mark/Mark Wahlberg would have said (if he stayed 'black').

Examples of People Who Give Off White Chocolate Vibes

1. Father Michael Pfleger, a genuinely great American pastor. One of the foremost important voices on many issues affecting the black community in Chicago, especially violence.

2. Prince Harry, second-generation royal swirler and credit to his race.

3. Angela Dorothea Merkel: Chancellor of Germany and perhaps the most prominent, committed and compassionate anti-racist leader of any Western nation. Whilst most Western leaders closed their borders and hearts to desperate refugees and migrants, she opened Germany's doors to one million of them ... and lost her job as a result.

4. Arsene Wenger, Britain's once most enthusiastic and persistent employer of black men.

5. Simon Albury, former CEO of the Royal Television Society and committed campaigner for greater diversity and real equal opportunities for black and other ethnic minorities in British broadcasting.

The Balanced Black Professional

Of course, in reality no one really fits into a single box (stereotype) all of the time. One size never fits all. We often move between different boxes, different characteristics and mannerisms, depending on the circumstances, or indeed how we feel that day. And it's the same for black professionals. Most black professionals are a dynamic composition of each of the black professional types detailed in previous chapters, with the honourable exception of white chocolate. (Unless, that is, you can pass for white. And if you can then you certainly should.)

They might adapt and adjust according to the situation they are facing, but at the core of it they are balanced. Like a good diet, they have all the right nutrients and a little something exciting on the side from time to time to keep things thrilling and just right for consumption. Following the balanced-diet analogy to its logical conclusion, most black professionals are what we (I, Dr Whytelaw) describe as 'balanced black professionals'.

The irony of the balanced black professional is this: what they project is balance, but what they tend to experience is anything but. As a result, they tend eventually to become, well, fairly imbalanced in the grand scheme of things.

The key thing the balanced black professional considers that he must do to go places in the corporate world is this: blend in. He tries to give the appearance of being comfortable in any surroundings and goes out of his way to make other people, white people, feel comfortable too. Not because he wants to, but because he has to.

So, the first thing to know about the balanced black professional is that he has two voices (not including the ones in his head). His public, professional, grandiose voice (or, in simple terms, his white voice, which can also be referred to as his government voice or nine-to-five voice) and his normal voice (sometimes referred to as his 'blackcent' or, as Senator Harry Reid would put it, 'his negro dialect').[18]

His white voice is an absolute necessity for him to get anywhere in the corporate world. A 'white-sounding voice' is, he

18 'Reid apologises for racial remarks about Obama during campaign', *CNN*, 10 January 2010.

hopes, the black professional's equivalent of a western pass-port: it opens doors without requiring a strenuous visa, affords comfort and shows that you're a good one. It's the sound of competence and professionalism. If white people must hear your voice, then it must sound like one of their better voices. Or else.

A white-sounding voice is the closest thing a black person has to what our homosexual brothers and sisters would call a closet. Somewhere or something that helps them hide their true identity in order to fulfil their potential without facing the burden or bigotry they would otherwise experience as a result of being 'out'.

However, unlike our homosexual brothers and sisters, no matter how far the balanced black professional may climb up the corporate ladder, he is not coming out of that closet anytime soon. To do so would be to risk absolute ruin.

Once he walks out of the office, however, he sighs, coughs twice, calls a friend and lets it all hang out. In fact, he lets rip. I'd insert an example but, on some G-shit you motherfuckers know what the fuck I'm talking about, yanadamean.

The balanced black professional, in his desire to blend in, will be easygoing. He knows he has to be liked, he wants to be loved, and naïvely he defines being loved as 'not being politi-cal'. He avoids the politics, doesn't strategise and isn't ruthless. Yet he is ambitious. He feels that sheer hard work, loyalty and, probably, prayer will propel him. Poor thang.

One of the key reasons why the balanced black professional does not engage or overinvest politically is that he feels, implic-itly or otherwise, that he cannot win. As a result, he gives up before he has even tried and simply hopes for the best. And works for the best too. But because he is overinvested in hard work and underinvested in politics, he goes nowhere fast and becomes frustrated and fatigued as a result.

THINK LIKE A WHITE MAN

The balanced black professional understands all of the hurdles facing him; he understands that what is a corporate ladder for most people is a corporate jungle for him. Why? Because he is black, and once you hit the age of about five or six you start to realise that something just isn't right.

But, as he is not speaking from the safe harbour of, say, a satirical book written by a coward under a pseudonym, he will never accept that he is facing hardship as a result of his blackness. He won't acknowledge racism, white privilege or skin colour-based structural institutional discrimination.

In a professional setting, this is good politics, for accepting that racism exists, giving it a name and challenging it, is to be shown the door. Of course, personally it's eating him up inside.

Yes, society (i.e. white people) be very grateful indeed that most black professionals are balanced black professionals. Because, if every black person was to take legal action (let alone LA Riots-style action) in the face of ethnicity-based prejudice or bigotry, the courts would have to run a 24-hour service in perpetuity.

Stiff Upper Lip

Ever wonder how the British developed their famed stiff upper lip?[19] The same way their popular music and their wealth was developed: they stole it from black people.

The stiff upper lip was one of the earlier forms of white cultural appropriation. Give it some thought: what adversity did the British face which required them to be restrained in

19 An admired quality in which one displays fortitude in the face of adversity or exercises great self-restraint in the expression of emotion.

their expression of emotion? The British inflicted adversity on others, especially people of African descent. The negro spiritual was the original stiff upper lip.

A stiff upper lip is the constant hallmark of the balanced black professional.

Real and normal-paced career progression takes place in two ways for the balanced black professional: either he moves around from firm to firm or he doesn't progress at all. A dead giveaway of the black professional is his curriculum vitae. Over a decade, most professionals will probably have worked in two, maybe three, roles. The balanced black professional will have worked in at least five. Probably five or six. Possibly more.

The likelihood is that the balanced black professional is job hopping for a number of reasons: he struggles with the politics (because, as we've seen already, it is a dirty business) and therefore he struggles to get promoted. Eventually he becomes angry, and rather than sitting in one place as he watches people with less ability and experience (but much better politics and whiter skin) leapfrog him, he moves on. And he does the same thing again and again. There is a good chance that it is the only way he will advance his career and the only way he'll secure any real power.

The problem for the balanced black professional, as a result of this career trajectory, is that he struggles to make any convincingly articulate long-term plans. It's hard to make long-term career plans when you're living day to day, month to month, cheque to cheque. Back to ground.

How Far Can He Go?

The sympathy vote doesn't reward like well-planned, well-executed, bloodthirsty, shrewdly ruthless politics, but it still gets you somewhere. Albeit slowly. So, the balanced black professional is likely to go as far as middle management.

There is another side to the balanced black professional's lack of political savvy. It's arguably the same reason why black people remained enslaved for so long and have not received reparations or apology for it till today: he is compassionate. Beyond reasonably. Often to his own detriment and to the benefit of his opposition.

His compassion, to some degree, fuels his good nature, which, sadly, in turn fuels his ruthless exploitation by others. But it also makes him give back abundantly to the community he emerged from. His compassion fuels his Helper Syndrome.

Hence, the balanced black professional will probably appear at schools and give advisory and cautionary talks, help out in the community, campaign on behalf of the next feelgood-nice-and-honest-almost-certainly-a-charlatan political movement.[20] But he is also likely to want to share his wisdom, knowledge, experience, compassion and cautionary tales with younger professionals and the community at large. Hence, he will also serve as a serial mentor and offer encouragement to others.

Gratitude and disdain should be shown to the balanced black professional in equal measure. For, without him, we, black people, would not be where we are today. And, because of him, we are exactly where are today.

---

20 For example, Dukakis '88, New Labour '97, Kerry/Vote or Die/ Anybody but Bush '04 and, of course, Obama '08, '12 and, if it was possible, '16, '20 and '24.

The Whytelaw Black Professional Type Risk Matrix Chart

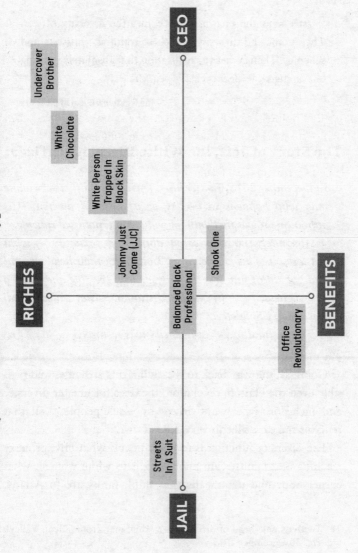

The Diversity Officer

'First comes the racism. Then comes the diversity officer. Then come the diversity speeches, training, statistics and schemes. Then comes the realisation that absolutely nothing has changed. Repeat cycle. Repeat cycle ...'

– The Whytelaw Cycle of Diversity

The Story of Jeff, the White Diversity Officer

In December 2015, Twitter hired Jeffrey Siminoff, a very white man who happens to be gay, as its head of diversity. His appointment was met with immediate international ridicule.[21]

Absolutely no one cared about his sexuality – what mattered was his ethnicity. So, Twitter got their head straight and got rid of him less than a year into the role and hired a – you guessed it – freckle-faced stunning sister called Candi Castleberry Singleton.[22]

The 'natural order' of diversity was restored.

Going all the way back to the civil rights struggles and possibly even the Haitian revolution, the cries for greater diversity and inclusion are always driven by black people. And that remains the case till this very day.

The diversity function is to black people what HR, primary teaching and mainstream publishing is to white women, what cornershops and deradicalisation think tanks are to Asians,

21 'Twitter's new head of diversity is a white man from Silicon Valley', *Quartz*, 30 December 2015.
22 'Twitter has a new VP of inclusion and diversity', *Techcrunch*, 27 June 2017.

and what everything else is to white men and White Men: their property. Everyone else is a guest.

Hence the diversity officer is a *de facto* black professional. Even if he or she is a white person, he or she remains a *de facto* black person, for the diversity officer is hired for the specific purpose of addressing and curtailing the fury of black people.

It is not unusual for the diversity officer to be the most senior black person in an organisation. In fact, it is the norm. And it is a dead giveaway that you're working for a stone-cold racist institution.

There are two types of diversity officer:

1. The diversity officer hired by accident.
2. The diversity officer hired correctly.

The Diversity Officer Hired by Accident

The diversity officer hired by accident is a good person with a good heart. A person who probably wakes up every morning listening to John Lennon's 'Imagine' while brushing her teeth. She was probably an activist in her younger life and hasn't really left those tendencies behind. She is someone who thinks that her role as a diversity officer is a great opportunity to make a real and substantive difference. To change the complexion and orientation of the organisation. And perhaps after that, the world!

In short, the diversity officer hired by accident is what is known in the real world, i.e. the white-dominated one outside her head, as a 'time waster'. She is wasting her time and everyone else's.

She doesn't understand her role at all. She was hired, literally, by accident. She believes her role is to make the organisation more diverse. In reality, her role is to serve as an off-site unofficial public relations outfit. Nothing more and nothing less.

She is there to manipulate and/or defend the 'diversity' statistics, yet she thinks she is there to enhance them. She is there to justify the actions of the organisation, yet she thinks she is there to challenge them. She is there to pacify and control ethnic minorities, yet she thinks she is there to empower them.

She will not last. Eventually she will leave or be managed out.

The Diversity Officer Hired Correctly

In order to effectively understand the diversity officer hired correctly, we must go back to more innocent times – 1991, to be precise.

In 1991, a white man called David Duke tried to become a White Man by running for governor of Louisiana as the Republican candidate. Duke 'happened' to be the former grand wizard of the KKK. And, for a Klansman, let alone a white guy, he 'happened' to be quite photogenic. So, for certain white voters, his appeal was clear: he had all of his teeth, he was vehemently racist, and he was white.

For black people, this was a nightmare come true: a leading Klansman as a viable contender for senator? This cannot be life.

The results came out. Duke got his flat white (supremacist) ass handed to him. Nevertheless, he won close to 40% of the total vote. And a strong majority of the white vote. Where things become interesting is that Duke won 2% of the black vote.

That's correct – Duke, a former grand wizard of the KKK with neo-Nazi ties, won 2% of all black voters.

This 2% is highly revealing. It unearths a well-hidden secret about black people. Some assumptions:

1. A quarter of the black people who voted for Duke were flat-out ignorant and, as such, didn't know what they were doing. They probably thought Duke was a lovely Justin Timberlake/David Attenborough-style white man.

2. Another quarter of those black people who voted for Duke were just trolling and/or being contrarian. They voted for an anti-black, extreme white supremacist as they thought it would be funny to do so.[23]

3. The other half of the 2% of black people who voted for Duke did it because they wanted him to win. And they wanted him to win for one sole reason: they hate black people.

That's correct: 1% of all black people harbour a deep-seated hatred of other black people. This manifests itself regularly. We call these people Black One-Percenters (or BOPs).

BOPs have nothing good to say about other black people. They automatically believe every single bad word that is said about a black person and they side with any form of oppression black people may be subject to. To all intent and purposes, BOPs harbour greater anti-black racism than even the most vehement David Duke-style racist.

BOPs make the best diversity officers. In fact, they make the best police chiefs.[24] The best supreme court judges. The best plantation overseers. Even the best *Fox News* contributors.[25]

Where an organisation finds a BOP – a one-in-a-hundred black person who just hates other black people – and is smart enough to appoint him/her as a diversity officer, that organisation will have no diversity issues to contend with ever again. BOP diversity officers know their role far too well. And will perform it with absolute gusto.

23 Not dissimilar to the 1,043,761 and 971,931 predominantly white people who voted in Boris Johnson for London Mayor in 2008 and 2012 respectively.

24 'Sheriff David Clarke Jr: the black Democrat who is Trump's favorite cop', *The Guardian*, 23 March 2017.

25 'Peterson: Trump Critics Claim "Racism" Because They're "Desperate" to Destroy Him', *Fox News*, 4 July 2017.

The BOP diversity officer is the correctly hired diversity officer. Yep, there is a 1% chance of finding her, but when the organisation does, it has struck gold. Black gold.

Examples of people who would make great diversity officers hired correctly: Jesse Lee Peterson, Bishop Abel Muzorewa, Uncle Ruckus, etc.

Key Risk Indicator Matrix for the Diversity Officer	
Risk Indicator	Score
Corporate star power (0 to 5)	Totally irrelevant
Ruthlessness level (0 to 5)	Totally irrelevant
Blackness level (-5 to 0)	Totally irrelevant but -5
Revolutionary tendency level (-5 to 0)	Totally irrelevant but 0
White lovability level (0 to 5)	Totally irrelevant
General political savvy (0 to 5)	Totally irrelevant
Overall potential in the white corporate world score	Absolutely, totally and entirely irrelevant
Black-on-black corporate association threat level	HIGHEST POSSIBLE

Risk Factor for Black Professionals

So what risk does the diversity officer – correctly and accidentally hired – pose to the ambitious black professional? Well, almost total. Once you're tagged as a person who needs the assistance of the diversity officer, it is hard to lose the stench.

It damages your (already fragile) brand as a beacon of competence and brilliance.

It is therefore prudent to totally avoid the diversity officer. The diversity function is often unstable and ill-respected. It is, at best, a public relations outfit and, at worst, the Klan in black face.

Say hello to them and keep moving.

The Black Boss

'I expect all of you to march with me and press on. (*Applause.*) Take off your bedroom slippers, put on your marching shoes. Shake it off. (*Applause.*) Stop complaining, stop grumbling, stop crying. We are going to press on. We've got work to do, Congressional Black Caucus. (*Applause.*)'

– President Barack Obama to the Congressional Black Caucus

The Story of Stan

From 2003 to 2007, Merrill Lynch[26] was headed up by a black man named Stan O'Neal, the grandson of an enslaved African. It goes without saying that this was an amazing achievement and he was paid eye-watering amounts of money. As Nelson Mandela famously said to Fidel Castro, 'Oh, how far we former slaves have come!'

But oh, how far we former slaves have to go.

During O'Neal's reign, a long-term employee named George McReynolds, who happened to be black, noticed clear discrepancies in opportunities and compensation for

26 Once a financial powerhouse, now defunct and swallowed up, in the main by Bank of America.

white employees as compared to black ones. He initially saw this in his office in Nashville, Tennessee (which evokes a 'duh' given the location). Laughably, he tried to resolve the matter internally but to no avail. So, in 2005, he did one of the whitest things known to man: he sued. He lawyered up, and it was on and cracking.

Initially, the case focused purely on McReynolds but, like a white Hollywood powerhouse facing sex abuse accusations, there were others. It eventually grew to include an estimated 1,200 employees, all alleging the same thing: black employees received lesser opportunities and pay than their white colleagues. All this time O'Neal was at the helm of the company.

In 2013, after eight years of slugging it out, Merrill Lynch put their hands up and accepted the facts. The case was settled out of court for $160m. A measly $1.5m less than they paid O'Neal himself to step down in 2007 (after running the company into the ground).

The key point is this: Merrill Lynch is more likely to be remembered as a meritocracy which gave the black grandson of a human slave the most powerful position in their company (albeit one who in turn damn near bankrupted the nation). Even though at the very same time, as it was eventually accepted, it was structured in a manner that yielded racist outcomes (pardon the cowardly diplomatic speak) for hundreds of its key black staff.

The black British political lobby[27] Operation Black Vote ran an article in July 2014 decrying the fact that, despite having a black managing director,[28] the British arm of the American

27 An extreme rarity in Britain.
28 Another extreme rarity in Britain.

postal service UPS appeared to 'struggle' with racism.[29] Black staff complained of being subjected to brazen racism; some even complained of the use of plantation and apartheid terminology, such as being called 'boy'. No report if anyone was nuked with the most enduring white invention of the last 500 years, the dreaded N-word.

This is not apartheid Johannesburg in the 80s or Mississippi in the 60s or Roseanne Barr's sleeping pills,[30] this is pre-Brexit lunacy, liberal multicultural Britain in 2014. A nation where fish and chips has long come second to the national favourite dish: Chicken Tikka Masala.

In one incident, Operation Black Vote reported, a presumably white senior manager turned to a black human resources manager while looking at a dreadlocked brother and said, 'We don't want any Rastafarians working here.'

And all this happened right under the nose of a black boss. How could this be?

This is actually a more common experience than you might think. It's the paradox of black professional life.

A black boss arrives and black professionals immediately believe that their lives will be enhanced. That black folk have finally risen to power. Here is someone who comes from the same type of background, ethnically at least, and presumably has a shared cultural connection, shared natural affinity and maybe a shared pain, including their experiences of the professional world. And as a result, black professionals are inspired, even a little in awe, seeing 'uncle, Dad, brother, aunt, Mum or sister' in the same way white people feel kinship with each other, too, especially in situations when they're in tiny numbers

29 'UPS: Race inequality rife despite black MD', *Operation Black Vote*, 29 July 2014.
30 'Roseanne Barr blames racist tweet on sleeping pills', *The Guardian*, 30 May 2018.

and surrounded. So, how could he, the black boss, not be the boss to make black professionals' lives that little bit easier by, at least, making the company a fairer and more egalitarian place?

Well, I'm afraid, the black boss may feel like Moses (or Marcus Mosiah Garvey) on arrival, but after a little while you'll quickly realise that he is Pharaoh (or George Bush Jnr). Far from letting his people go, he is personally blowing up the levees. As opposed to bettering your experience in the office, he may actually make it much worse.

This is naturally one of the most disappointing aspects of black professional life. If the black boss is not going to level the playing field, then who will? Rhetorical question, obviously. The answer is: the White Man. When the interests of the White Man are threatened enough, things change ... into another form.

But why does this happen? Why doesn't the black boss separate the Red Sea and lead the metaphorical exodus of corporate shenanigans that often consign fellow black professionals to the garbage heap? Well, there are multiple reasons. Below are a few.

The Black Boss Is Not an Activist Either

From the top, perhaps the main reason why the black boss disappoints (from a black perspective) boils down to good old-fashioned unrealistic expectations.

The black boss, like any boss, has been hired to deliver a specific set of outcomes and he will be assessed against those outcomes and remunerated accordingly. The likelihood of the black boss being set some black agenda outcomes within the predominantly white corporate structure is laughably unrealistic yet seemingly widely expected.

The black boss is not there to be Toussaint Louverture or Assata Shakur. He is there to be Bernie Madoff (hopefully without the extreme kleptomania) or Charles Montgomery 'Monty' Burns. In black face.

And, like any other black professional, he may have an impressive job title but he is still a black person. Precious little will end his career faster than engaging in a mini-civil rights struggle.

In short, he is not an activist. He is just another boss. Expecting something different from him is ludicrous.

Vetted for White Power

Unless the corporation is either totally incompetent or clearly about to go bust, then the black boss would have been meticulously vetted. There is no way in a million years that a black person with a radical, revolutionary, reformist or even mildly active anti-racist bone in his body is going to be allowed to acquire any real power in the corporation. The objective is to increase profits or to start making a profit (unless you work for a charity or some form of tax-dependent blood-sucking organisation such as the police) and the last thing they need is some pseudo Che Guevara metaphorically disassembling and reassembling his AK-47 daily in the dark (maybe in the stationery cupboard).

If they are going to place power in black hands, they will want to find the most stable pair of black hands they can get. If they can't find a stable pair of black hands, they'll find a good old reliable pair of white hands. The only real way the black boss can let the powers that be know that he is a stable pair of hands is by letting them see the mirror image of themselves when they look at him.

When the CEO of a company[31] starts wearing a different type of suit, shortly afterwards his minions start to do the same. Monkey see, monkey do.

For example, when incarcerated White Man Jeffrey Skilling, the former CEO of Enron, got laser surgery on his eyes, a number of his fellow executives apparently followed suit. The bigger the money, the bigger the monkey.

The black boss will want to send out all the right signals in order to inspire confidence in him. Even if that means having to render the black professional collateral damage in the process.

Autopilot

By the time a company is willing to 'risk' placing power in black hands, it is a sure sign that white privilege, white supremacy and Elvis is King-ism are firmly on autopilot. Either that, or the corporation is about to sink (and all corporations eventually sink). Usually both. But for the purpose of this section, let's address the former.

Most people of any ethnicity don't really know or understand what equality really is because inequality is the perfectly conceivably realistic norm. Equality is a radically alien concept that is often the preserve of Bob Dylan-loving, white radical debates. Key word: *debates*.

Gender inequality, for example, is perfectly normal. It's 'normal' for men to hold power, privilege and the purse. And it is normal for women to be seen as trophy wives, pretty accessories, 'secret weapons' (usually to very powerful men, especially politicians), earth mother types or, well, hoes.

A woman who really understands inequality and embarks on smashing the glass ceiling (the patriarchy, the old boys'

31 Notice how a pale male being popped into your conscience.

network, the White Man racket and so on), goes for hers and shows ruthless determination and unapologetic authentic solidarity with other women (in word and deed) is deemed an extreme-feminist careerist – let's keep it real, a bitch. A threat to something called 'our way of life', that is, the White Man's way of life.

The key clause in the narrative above is 'unapologetically showing authentic solidarity with other women (in word and deed)'. The 'natural order of things', i.e. the self-preserving and perpetuating White Man power structure, would, and does, accommodate the odd ambitious (usually white) woman coming along and joining the power structure – provided she comes alone and on their terms in order to further their cause.

In this regard, things for white women in high places are similar to those for the black professional. By the time the company is 'ready' to appoint a black boss, the terms of reference are set, the game is rigged, and the rules are clear: 'This is how things work over here, you should feel privileged to be here, and if you want to remain here then this is exactly how you will have to continue to behave.'

Of course, these words are never spoken. Or written. Until now. But they're always understood. By the time a black professional is ready to assume some degree of power, then it means that they have received the message above loud and clear.

Obama 2012

'The noisy wheel gets the grease' is the old saying. 'If you don't ask, you don't get' is perhaps more common. When it comes to the black boss, black professionals are often guilty of both: not asking and not being noisy. This allows the black boss to get away with doing nothing for fellow black professionals.

The likelihood of black professionals coordinating, organising and potentially moving against him is as realistic as John Bolton and Hassan Rouhani eloping in a happy gay union. Therefore, they pose no risk, no threat and no bother. So why even bother?

Part of the reason why black professionals don't trouble the black boss is simply because they have a clear understanding of what he has been through to get to where he is. They see their own struggle, hopes and aspirations embodied in what he has achieved. He is a symbol of their dreams. And yes, you can't 'eat' symbolism but symbolism is a necessary part of the human experience.

'If he can do it, then so can I.'

We see strength in ourselves through the achievements and triumphs of others like us. It's this base psychology that makes white people construct and clutch onto fictional heroes in their image; the white Jesus prototype is the most obvious example of this, with Elvis a close second.

In addition to knowing where they have come from, black professionals know exactly what the black boss is up against: the same thing that they're up against. Perhaps even a more exaggerated and aggressive version. So, as opposed to holding him to account or threatening to walk unless he betters their condition, they do nothing. Nothing but hope that, once he gets comfortable and has nothing to lose, he will be more than able to help them out. Once he gets comfortable everything will be all right.

Some would call this concept the illusion of inclusion. More contemporary thinkers would call it the 'illusion of the second term', or, for simplicity, Obama 2012.

'It'll be different next time' is the hope. The reality is that it may get worse. Much worse.

The White Man's Diversity Indemnity
Insurance Policy

Even the foremost racist, or institutionally racist, of companies or organisations have a need to ensure that they don't *appear* so. It's a new day – no corporation wants to be mistaken for the Ku Klux Klan. Not even the Ku Klux Klan.[32]

No company wants to be caught out when some angry, nosy bedroom blogger starts asking about the number of black people on their payroll. Diversity, even at its least sincere, shuts down criticism, creates good public relations, and gives the company a ring of modernity and progressiveness. In short, it makes them seem like nice people. Nice, cosy, dessert-cheese-eating white liberals.

But when a company has a black boss, it doesn't need to hire a single other black person to appear diverse and progressive. He is a one-man diversity and progressiveness billboard, both qualitatively and quantitatively. He is the White Man's billboard.

'How can America be racist if it has a black president?' There is a good chance you heard those words between 2009 and 2017.

When you've hired a black boss, the company doesn't need to go to the 'painful' lengths of creating a veneer of respectability by being progressive and diverse. That's what they pay the black boss for. He does that for them. He is the silver, hollow-tip diversity bullet.

32 'The Ku Klux Klan opens its door to Jews, homosexuals and black people in bizarre recruitment drive', *Daily Mail*, 10 November 2014.

Famous Black Bosses

1. Channing Dungey, principled President of ABC who risked her own job by firing a popular racist at the height of her ratings popularity. Rare senior black person in media who is not a diversity officer.

2. Barack Obama, founding pillar of Obamamania and focal point of Yes We Can.

3. Stringer Bell (*The Wire*), highly innovative and forward-thinking leader of young men. Ruthless at hiring and firing. Totally against nepotism.

4. Reginald Lewis, the first black billionaire and author of *Why Should White Guys Have All The Fun?*.

5. Stan O'Neal, black Machiavelli and the most senior black person in Wall Street history.

The Whytelaw Corporate Negro Test

So, now that you have read all of the profiles (stereotypes), you're probably wondering what type of black professional you are. The test below is a swift way to find out what role you play in the grand scheme of white corporatism. In addition to finding out exactly who you are, this test is also a good chance to check how calibrated you are in terms of thinking like a White Man.

When the White Man looks at you, does he think:

   a) If it all goes down, this one will be an asset to me?

   b) If it all goes down, this one will be a huge problem?

   c) If it all goes down, this one will be of no consequence?

   d) If it all goes down, I'm not sure if this one will be an asset or a problem?

   e) Thanks to confused cowardly hearts like this one, it will never go down!?

Answers:

   If **a)** You're an undercover brother or a black boss.

   If **b)** You're an office revolutionary or streets in a suit.

   If **c)** You're JJC, white chocolate or a diversity officer.

   If **d)** You're a balanced black professional.

   If **e)** You're a white person 'trapped' in black skin or a shook one.

Appendix 2

White Man Decoded:
The Black Professional's Dictionary

'You start out in 1954 by saying, "Nigger, nigger, nigger."
By 1968 you can't say "nigger" – that hurts you. Backfires.
So, you say stuff like "forced busing", "states' rights" and all
that stuff. You're getting so abstract now [that] you're talking
about cutting taxes, and all these things you're talking about
are totally economic things and a by-product of them is [that]
blacks get hurt worse than whites. And subconsciously maybe
that is part of it. I'm not saying that. But I'm saying that if it is
getting that abstract, and that coded, that we are doing away
with the racial problem one way or the other. You follow me
– because obviously sitting around saying, "We want to cut
this," is much more abstract than even the busing thing, and
a hell of a lot more abstract than "Nigger, nigger".'

**– dead White Man Lee Atwater, political consultant and campaign
manager for George W. Bush's successful presidential campaign (1988)**

L inguistic warfare is, I pray, the last stand of the White
Man (especially in the corporate setting). It is critical for
every black professional to understand exactly what the
White Man really means when he uses a somewhat vague and
innocent-sounding term. To help out, opposite is a dictionary of
popularly used coded terms.

What the White Man says	What the White Man really means
The West	White people
The international community	White people
The good people of the world	White people
The civilised world	White people
The silent majority	White people
The free world	White people
Family of nations	White people
Ordinary people	White people
Real people	White people
Working class	White people
Middle America	White people
Middle England	White people
Middle income	White people
Middle class	White people
White people	White people
Shy Trump voter	White people. And a third of Latinos.
Brexiteer	White people and people who have mistaken themselves for white people.
Our allies	White people Nations who do the bidding of white people, often against their own interests. See 'good black leader', 'Arab king' and 'benevolent dictator'.
Leader of the free world	A White Man (or pseudo White Man) who directly leads a government for, by and of white people.
Foreign government	A government white people like.
Regime	A government white people don't particularly like but in some instances may tolerate. Usages: first comes the 'regime', then comes the call for 'regime' change and then comes the 'regime changer'.

What the White Man says	What the White Man really means
Stable/good regime	An authoritarian, torturing hellhole of a state which sells its natural resources to white people cheaply and then buys expensive weapons from white people in return. Or else.
Unstable/bad regime	An authoritarian, torturing hellhole of a state which sells its natural resources to the Chinese and Hollywood-villain white people cheaply and then buys expensive weapons from China and Hollywood-villain white people in return which makes real white people very unhappy.
Regime change	White people have had enough of a particular black or brown leader/king/dictator/ophthalmologist and have therefore decided to drop tons of bombs and high explosives on said person's country in order to destroy him (and maybe a few hundred thousand innocent civilians).
Dictator	National-level leader white people don't like. Sometimes a king, sometimes a general, sometimes an ophthalmologist, sometimes even democratically elected.
Strong man	An authoritarian leader white people don't particularly like but will begrudgingly do business with as he favours their interests. *Example*: Mugabe after the fall of Rhodesia and before Tony Blair and Clare Short violated the Lancaster House agreement.[1]
Black Hitler	Strong man or dictator in the extreme. A foreign, inevitably black, leader, usually African, who white people cannot stand because he champions the interests of his own people (usually via a Swiss bank account or two) over theirs. *Example*: Mugabe after Tony Blair and Clare Short violated the Lancaster House agreement.
Terrorist	A Muslim or, at the very least, brown person, who white people perceive to be an extreme and deranged irrational threat.

1 'I should make it clear that we do not accept that Britain has a special responsibility to meet the costs of land purchase in Zimbabwe. We are a new Government from diverse backgrounds without links to former colonial interests. My own origins are Irish and as you know we were colonised not colonisers.' – Clare Short's 1997 letter to the Mugabe-led Zimbabwean government while Secretary of State for International Development (1997–2003).

What the White Man says	What the White Man really means
Terrorism	A Muslim or, at the very least, brown person, waging acts of extreme violence for political reasons. It should be noted that white people are never capable of committing 'terrorism'.
Domestic terrorism	White people waging acts of extreme violence for political reasons. It should be noted that black, brown and/or Muslim people are never capable of committing 'domestic terrorism'.
Not thought to be terror-related	'White people have been killed in large numbers in a violent, politically motivated attack, however, the culprit is white … So, nothing to worry about.'
Collateral damage	An innocent and blameless dead black or brown person who died as a result of white people's military objectives (see regime change). Opposite: terror victim.
Campaign/mission	Mass violence against black and brown people which aims to steal their resources but is likely to be chalked up to democracy. 'Our *campaign* in Pipelineria was highly successful. The oil fields have been secured. *Mission* accomplished. Democracy blooms.'
Muslim	Deranged brown person (sometimes mistaken for Hindus), who pose an extreme threat to white people.
Moderate Muslim	Deranged brown person (sometimes mistaken for a Buddhist), who poses a moderate to mild threat to white people.
Black leader	A black person who provides intellectual, social and, inevitably, spiritual guidance to black people in order to 'fill the void' left by white people.
Bad black leader	A black person who agitates for change and the toppling of the power structure that currently benefits white people. Sometimes disparagingly referred to as a cleric. *Examples*: fat Al Sharpton and imprisoned Nelson Mandela.
Good black leader	A black person who, perhaps inadvertently, keeps black people in check on behalf of white people. Sometimes disparagingly referred to as a turncoat. *Examples*: slim Al Sharpton and President Nelson Mandela.
Very good black leader	A dead black leader who white people can evoke, selectively, to suit their own purposes. Never knowingly underquoted. *Examples*: Al Sharpton (when he meets his maker) and dead Nelson Mandela.

What the White Man says	What the White Man really means
World leader	A White Man who leads a country dominated by white people.
Middle East	A place white people intend to bomb or are actively bombing.
	A very large petrol station for white people.
	Arabland – a fictional place created by white people 'where they'll chop off your hands if they don't like your face!'
	Agrabah[2] – a fictional place created by white people which 30% of Republican voters (i.e. white people) would happily bomb.
Africa	The White Man's burden to white people's benefit.
	A place where white people get natural resources, often for free. Including the original natural resource: black people.
	A place where white people go to launder their consciences and do good. But usually end up doing quite well.
	'The dark continent', a vast, bad, and scary place for white people.
	A place where white people conduct political, economic, social and medical experiments. And sometimes even sexual experiments.
	A place where the Chinese are posing a serious threat to the hegemony of white people.
	A place where white people are unable to walk an average street alone, yet emerge as TV newsworthy experts after being there for a few hours.
	A place where black people make up the majority of the population and white people make up the majority of TV news experts.
	A place where white people go for a few days and attain lucrative book/TV documentary deals for doing so.
	A continent where the fate of tusk-bearing animals is considered by white people to be of much greater concern than the fate of human beings.
	A continent sliced, diced and named by white people.

2 'Poll: 30% of GOP voters support bombing Agrabah, the city from Aladdin', *The Guardian*, 18 December 2015.

APPENDIX 2

What the White Man says	What the White Man really means
Liberalise your economy	Gracefully bend over for white people so they can fleece your nation of its resources – at fire sale prices.
International law	Laws created by white people, and often violated by white people, but only ever enforced (in court) against black (African) people.
International Criminal Court	A court created by white people which only ever tries black African people.
War crimes	Serious criminality conducted in the process of war that white people would have you believe only black and brown people commit. And only white people can punish.
Heroic acts of patriotic duty	War crimes committed by white people.
Democracy	White people's sacredly favoured form of government.
	A weapon white people bash around the heads of people they don't like, even if they're democratically elected.
	An obstacle to white people doing good business.
	A pretext used by white people to wage war and seize control of a nation's natural resources.
Black person	Person who scares and intimidates white people.
	Person who entertains white people.
	Person enslaved by white people.
	Person outside demonstrating against white people.
	Person who probably has more than a few white people in his or her ancestry.
Angry black person	Black person who knows what the hell is going on and is therefore considered a serious threat to white people.
Rhodes	An extremely lovely man and purveyor of academic scholarships – to white people. A murdering white supremacist maniac – to black people.
Leopold	An extremely lovely man – to white people. A murdering white supremacist maniac – to black people.
Fascism	White people doing to other white people what white people have been doing to black people for centuries.
Racism	White people doing their thing.

What the White Man says	What the White Man really means
Reverse racism	Corrective action against racism which leaves white people immensely angry, as it curtails their ability to do their thing.
'Economic anxiety'[3]	White people doing their thing. Synonym: racism.
Hostile environment[4]	Racist environment. White people doing their thing. Synonym: Jim Crow.
Identity politics	Corrective action against racism (and other -isms and phobias) which leaves certain white people immensely angry as it curtails their ability to do their thing.
Reparations	A topic white people have no interest in discussing, defining or determining. And certainly not paying.
Benevolent dictator	Dictator white people like but who runs a fairly decent public relations machine.
Community leader	A non-white person hand-picked by white people in the media – usually following a major crisis – to speak on behalf of the race- or religion-based community (invariably black or brown) he or she has emerged from (or was selected to speak on behalf of). It should be noted that once he/she says anything white people do not like, then said community leader will be stripped of their privileges and banished to the wilderness (blogs, Twitter and the comments sections of newspapers). Someone who is recognised by a community as a leader, outside the realm of democratic politics, who is able to speak for the community (to white people) or explain white-people stuff to the community. A conduit or whisperer of sorts.
Black politician X is a 'uniting figure'	Black politician X would be politically, economically and socially good for white people. And he would take lots of selfies with black people.

3 'TRUMP VOTERS' ECONOMIC ANXIETY HAS MAGICALLY DISAPPEARED', *Vanity Fair*, 17 April 2017.
4 A set of policy measures created by the British government to make the UK as uncomfortable a place as possible for people without the right papers. Ultimately led to the harassment and deportation of people without the right skin colour.

What the White Man says	What the White Man really means
Black politician X is a 'divisive figure'	Black politician X would be politically, economically and socially good for black and other marginalised people (as opposed to just white people).
Gentrification	When white people feel that it is high time that a black neighbourhood belongs to them. When Rastafarians are thrown out by trustafarians.
Urban area	An area white people either intend to gentrify or are currently gentrifying.
Suburban area	An area where white people live in peace and harmony away from non-white people.
Assimilate and integrate	'Shut up, sit up and act like white people. Or else.'
Mistakes	Regrettable errors that white people are allowed to learn from and black people are defined by, imprisoned for or killed for.
'We need to have an open and honest debate about racism, immigration, the black experience'	When white people want the ability to be at their most virulently racist without a remote hint of repercussion.
Freedom of speech	The right to say whatever you want, provided it is not too insulting, offensive or threatening to white people. White people's right to be flagrantly racist and dehumanising towards non-white people without a hint of repercussion.
Neighbourhood watch	White people with a few small guns.
NRA	White people with medium-sized guns.
NATO	White people with massive guns.
Migrant	Black or brown person moving to a historically white country for lowly paid, better economic opportunities. White people find this very displeasing.
Expat	White person moving to a historically white or black or yellow or red or brown country for highly paid, better economic opportunities. White people tend not to mind this.

THINK LIKE A WHITE MAN

What the White Man says	What the White Man really means
Great orator	Demagogue who says what white people like hearing.
Demagogue	Great orator who says what white people don't like hearing.
Thug	Nigger.

Credits

Conceiving, creating and publishing a racially spiced non-fiction satirical self-help book[1] can only really be compared to creating and promoting a top-notch gangsta rap album. I bringeth receipts:

Below is the roll call of the amazing talent who helped bring *Think Like a White Man* to life, based on the credits of the single greatest piece of art ever created in the western hemisphere: Snoop Dogg's first album, *Doggystyle*.

Please be assured that no one was shot, shanked or seduced in the creation of this book.

If *Think Like a White Man* was made by Death Row Records (in its risqué heyday)		
Death Row personnel	*Think Like a White Man* equivalent personnel	Role, responsibilities, characteristics & achievements
Snoop Doggy Dogg	Dr Boulé Whytelaw III, *voice of a generation.*	Unique, refreshing, forthright and extremely appealing talent. Firmly anti-establishment, eternally young, wild & free. Prone to reinventing himself.
Dr Dre	Nels Abbey, *writer.*	Ground-breaking innovator and (currently underpaid) extraordinarily excellent producer of great art. The most bankable creative of his time. Defiant. Above all, modest.

1 A genre of one.

Suge Knight	Hannah Knowles, *editor.*	Double OG. Brains, power and muscle all wrapped up into a fearless risk-taker. Unapologetically champions black creatives (and the black arts) but not averse to 'ruthlessly getting rid of/cutting rubbish'. A real-life Vito Corleone.
David Kenner	Julia Kingsford, *agent (and therapist).*	The grown-up in the room. Consigliere to all sides. Committed to the success of the creative and keeping them out of jail. Sharp as a serpent, gentle as a dove. Mafioso-ish.
Nate Dogg	Kate E, *creative advisor.*	Unfadeable unique purveyor of tasteful artistic expression and calming presence who helps push every product they're involved in from good to great. Somehow makes 'political incorrectness' sound so… sweet. Feminist.
Tha Dogg Pound, DJ Sal T Nuttz, DJ Eaz-E-Dick, Taa-Dow, the staff of W-Ballz[2] and assorted gangbangers.	The Brotherhood, *inspiration (and frustration).*	A collective of highly intelligent, argumentative, meme-savvy, (self-) righteous and successful brothers offering tales straight from survival scrolls, deep thoughts and information on affairs of the day relevant to the subject matter.
The DOC	Alison Rae, *copyeditor.*	OG. Steps in to ensure everything sounds right and tight. Suggests enhancements where it can sound better.
Warren G	Lydia Yadi, *talent discoverer[3] and adviser.*	Cool-as-an-air conditioner gentle soul who identified and initially developed the talent only for the treacherous talent to be absorbed by a different organisation. Remains a friend and adviser.
Lil Bow Wow	Lil Nay Nay (aka Naomi[4]), *inadvertent collaborator and inspiration.*	Forthright youngster who won't leave the studio/study so ends up contributing to art they're far too young to consume.

2 187.4 FM
3 Please note that in this instance the term 'discoverer' is not intended to invoke thoughts of Christopher Columbus and small pox blankets.
4 Ages of zero to four.

George 'Papa G' Pryce	Anna Frame, *publicity & communications.* Jenny Fry,	Slick-as-oil industry legends who develop creative ways to ensure everyone is aware of the 'amazing' product and deal with all media manoeuvring.
Joe Cool, Kimberly Holt.	Kate Oliver, Ed Pickford, Gill Heeley, Nishant Choksi *production, design and cover art.*	Geniuses of the visual arts who made this piece of art look and feel like something you must own.
George Clinton, Lady of Rage, Jewell and Daz Dillinger.	Ashley Clark, Natalie Carter, Sinmi Kalejaiye and Rukaiya Russell. *Early feedback providers.*	Critical people to the creation process. Provided critical feedback and input at a very early stage.
Michael 'Harry-O' Harris	'Harry-Kay E', *silent partner.*	Shadowy hand who helped establish the creative endeavour at inception. Offers material support and encouragement to keep going when all hope seemed lost. Only ever one call away.
Sharitha Knight	Vicki Rutherford, *managing editor.*	The Rolls Royce engine under the bonnet who ensures the product is made to an exceptionally high standard and everyone meets their deadlines. Extremely business-like … and extremely professional. Iron fist in a vintage velvet glove.
Jimmy Iovine & Ted Fields	Jamie Byng, *shot caller.*	Triple OG. Passion-driven maverick extraordinaire behind countless classics and blockbusters. Greenlights, funds and promotes the entire show. Never afraid of the two Cs: creativity and controversy. Defiant one.

To everyone mentioned above: your hands are as bloody as mine! Till the wheels fall off, till the casket drops: thank you.

Dr Boulé Whytelaw
Somewhere, 2019

Acknowledgements

Never in a month of post-racial Sundays did I think that *Think Like a White Man* would see the light of day and be in your hands right now.

I set out on what I considered to be a ridiculously futile mission: to write the blackest book possible – and, if possible, the blackest book ever. Something so ludicrously and universally black it would be just too alarmingly black[5] for Britain (even Croydon). Something you wouldn't expect to read this side of the Rhodesian Bush War.

I was eager to ensure that it didn't contain any of the usual (and very necessary) nuances, sensitivities, clichés and romantic lies that are part and parcel of our conversations around surviving racism, and excelling despite racism. Yep, *surviving*.

Just as importantly I set out to write something that would document the experience of the day, serve as personal therapy as well as make me (and, hopefully, you) laugh, cringe, think and then do better.

All the above, I believe, was accomplished. But it was only accomplished with the help of many people to whom I owe an irredeemable debt of gratitude, they are:

- Canongate Books. Thanks so much for being creative, courageous and crazy enough to believe in *Think Like a White Man*, take it on board and push it to success. Huge thanks to Jamie Byng, the indefatigable Hannah Knowles,

5 After nearly 2000 mentions I suspect you've had enough of the words 'black' and 'white' for one life time so these will be the last mentions.

Jenny Fry, Anna Frame, Vicki Rutherford, Aa'Ishah Hawton and Alison Rae.

- Penguin Random House. Thank you for establishing the WriteNow programme that helped me (and many others) so much. Special thanks to Lydia Yadi, Morwenna Loughman, Siena Parker, Rebecca Smart and Tom Weldon.

- Kingsford & Campbell. Julia Kingsford: you are bloody amazing. Thanks for your patience, passion, integrity, calming nature and all your work.

- Advisers. Thanks to Kirsty Lang, James Scudamore, Misha Glenny, Reni Eddo-Lodge, Nikesh Shukla, Elizabeth Cochrane and the Big Green Bookshop for all of your time, concern and advice on the publishing world.

- Feedbackers. Thanks to Natalie Carter, Sinmi Kalejaiye, Ashley Clark, Elijah Lawal, John Edwards[6], Elizabeth 'Biz' Pears, Ronke & Nolitha Olusanya. Your open and honest feedback proved priceless.

- The Brotherhood. A huge RNDRT to: Deji Bakare ('and the aftermath is ...'), Sheyi 'BO Telly' Teluwo, Chris 'The Tory' Frimpong, Christian 'Cobblahnomics' Cobblah, Mohammed Kamara, Lanre Adebola, Prince Kwakye, Femi Cole, Mustafa Akindele, Pervell Jecty (wesseeya for leeya, neeya), Jermaine Atie, Salman 'Hollywood' Ahmed, David 'DJT' Tullett, Peter '50' Gabriels, Jerome 'liberalism' Danvers, Ansu Bai-Marrow. Let's keep realising our dreams.

- Special thanks to Ade Adeluwoye, Marcelle Moncrieffe Johnson, Dr Rob Berkeley MBE, Serra Tezisler, Jasmine Dotiwala, Symeon Brown, Pat Younge, Vijay Patel, Andrew Stalker, Cebo Luthuli, Aaron Akinyemi, Derek Owusu &

6 John: thanks for pointing out that Samuel Beckett is a 'good one'.

all the brothers who contributed to Safe, Tommy Nagra, Sarah Milad, Maurice Mcleod, Ade Solanke, Hannah Kamara, the entire Media Diversified crew, Elonka Soros, the Playahata squad, Courttia Newland, the 2017 WriteNow intake, George Ruddock, Steve Pope & the *Voice* newspaper, the *Evening Standard*.

- Huge thanks to my entire family: Mum, Dad, Dennis, Paul & Esohe, Alero, Eyitemi, Vivienne, Odun & Funmi, Faith, Segun & Funmi, Victor, Tosan & Tolu. Sinmi, Jemine & Phillipe, Temi, Lotunda, Sikama & Sola, Oscar & Beverly. Georgia and Jason. Ernest & Ingrid. John & Ruth. Richard, Laura, Ellie & Alex, Stefano, Deji, Mel and the Bakare family. Sheyi, Felicia, Mummy and the Teluwo family, Chris & Tarita, Stella, Frank & the Ajilore family. Anna, Bruno & Joshua & the Edenogie family.

- Kate & Naomi. My girls, my gang. My mentors, my tormentors. Thank you for everything and for being my everything.

Finally, God: without the gentle and guiding hand of, I'd be in the firm and immobilising grip of the system. And for that I'm forever thankful.

Nels,
London, 2019